Teacher Edition

Reveal
MATH™
Language Development
Handbook

Course 1

Mc
Graw
Hill
Education

my.mheducation.com

Send all inquiries to:
McGraw-Hill Education
STEM Learning Solutions Center
8787 Orion Place
Columbus, OH 43240

ISBN: 978-0-07-697589-1 *(Language Development Handbook, Course1, Teacher Edition)*
MHID: 0-07-697589-4 *(Language Development Handbook, Course1, Teacher Edition)*
ISBN: 978-0-07-902924-9 *(Language Development Handbook, Course 1, Student Edition)*
MHID: 0-07-902924-8 *(Language Development Handbook, Course 1, Student Edition)*

Visual Kinesthetic Vocabulary® is a registered trademark of
Dinah-Might Adventures, LP.

1 2 3 4 5 6 7 8 9 10 LKV 27 26 25 24 23 22 21 20 19 18

Contents

McGraw-Hill Education's Guiding Principles for Supporting English Learners

McGraw-Hill Education is committed to providing English Learners appropriate support as they simultaneously learn content and language. As an organization, we recognize that the United States is a culturally and linguistically diverse country. Moreover, this diversity continues to increase, with corresponding growth in the number of English Learners (ELLs). In 2012–2013, an estimated 4.85 million ELLs were enrolled US schools; this subgroup now makes up nearly 10% of the total public school enrollment (Ruiz-Soto, Hooker, and Batalova, 2015). In fact, ELLs are the fastest growing student population in the country, growing 60% in the last decade, compared with only 7% growth of the general student population (Grantmakers for Education, 2013). Perhaps most interesting of all, the vast majority of ELLs – 85% of prekindergarten through fifth grade ELLs, and 62% of high school ELLs – were born in the United States (Zong & Batalova, 2015). These US-born ELLs may be first-, second-, or third-generation students with strong ties to their cultural roots.

A great many ELLs come to school with a variety of rich linguistic and cultural backgrounds from Spanish-speaking communities and countries all throughout the Americas. In addition to Spanish, there are some ELLs that come to school speaking fluent or limited Spanish in addition to an indigenous language native to North, Central and South America. In addition, schools experience native speakers from numerous other backgrounds and languages—the most common other languages being Cantonese, Hmong, Korean, Vietnamese, and Haitian Creole. While over 70% of ELLs come to school speaking Spanish as their native language, as a group, ELLs speak nearly 150 languages (Baird, 2015). The experiences and identities acquired in the context of ELLs' homes and communities can transform the simplest classroom into a unique cultural and linguistic microcosm.

English Learners' success in learning a second language is influenced by a variety of factors besides the instructional method itself, including individual, family, and classroom characteristics; school and community contexts; the attributes of the assessment used to measure progress; and whether the language acquired is a national or foreign language (August & Shanahan, 2006; Genesee, Lindholm-Leary, Saundes, & Christian, 2006). For instance, children's initial levels of proficiency in their home language(s), along with English, influence new language acquisition (August, Shanahan, Escamilla, K., 2009) as does the quality of school support (Niehaus & Adelson, 2014) and the characteristics of the language learners' first and second languages (Dressler & Kamil, 2006)

Given these factors, there is a pressing need for fundamental principles that guide the support of ELLs as they acquire content and develop language. Drawing upon extensive research in the field, McGraw-Hill Education has developed nine guiding principles for supporting English Learners at all grade levels and in all disciplines.

Guiding Principles

- ✓ Provide Specialized Instruction

- ✓ Cultivate Meaning

- ✓ Teach Structure and Form

- ✓ Develop Language in Context

- ✓ Scaffold to Support Access

- ✓ Foster Interaction

- ✓ Create Affirming Cultural Spaces

- ✓ Engage Home to Enrich Instruction

- ✓ Promote Multilingualism

Proficiency Level Descriptors

	Interpretive (Input)		Productive (Output)	
	Listening	Reading	Writing	Speaking
An Entering/Emerging Level ELL • New to this country; may have memorized some everyday phrases like, "Where is the bathroom", "My name is....", may also be in the "silent stage" where they listen to the language but are not comfortable speaking aloud • Struggles to understand simple conversations • Can follow simple classroom directions when overtly demonstrated by the instructor	• Listens actively yet struggles to understand simple conversations • Possibly understands "chunks" of language; may not be able to produce language verbally	• Reads familiar patterned text • Can transfer Spanish decoding somewhat easily to make basic reading in English seem somewhat fluent; comprehension is weak	• Writes labels and word lists, copies patterned sentences or sentence frames, one- or two-word responses	• Responds non-verbally by pointing, nodding, gesturing, drawing • May respond with yes/no, short phrases, or simple memorized sentences • Struggles with non-transferable pronunciations.
A Developing/Expanding Level ELL • Is dependent on prior knowledge, visual cues, topic familiarity, and pretaught math-related vocabulary • Solves word problems with significant support • May procedurally solve problems with a limited understanding of the math concept.	• Has ability to understand and distinguish simple details and concepts of familiar/ previously learned topics	• Recognizes obvious cognates • Pronounces most English words correctly, reading slowly and in short phrases • Still relies on visual cues and peer or teacher assistance	• Produces writing that consists of short, simple sentences loosely connected with limited use of cohesive devices • Uses undetailed descriptions with difficulty expressing abstract concepts	• Uses simple sentence structure and simple tenses • Prefers to speak in present tense.
A Bridging Level ELL • May struggle with conditional structure of word problems • Participates in social conversations needing very little contextual support • Can mentor other ELLs in collaborative activities.	• Usually understands longer, more elaborated directions, conversations, and discussions on familiar and some unfamiliar topics • May struggle with pronoun usage	• Reads with fluency, and is able to apply basic and higher-order comprehension skills when reading grade-appropriate text	• Is able to engage in writing assignments in content area instruction with scaffolded support • Has a grasp of basic verbs, tenses, grammar features, and sentence patterns	• Participates in most academic discussions on familiar topics, with some pauses to restate, repeat, or search for words and phrases to clarify meaning.

Collaborative Conversations

Students engage in whole-class, small-group, and partner discussions during every lesson. The chart below provides prompt frames and response frames that will help students at different language proficiency levels interact with each other in meaningful ways.

You may wish to post these frames in the classroom for student reference.

Core Skills	Prompt Frames	Response Frames
Elaborate and Ask Questions	Can you tell me more about it? Can you give me some details? Can you be more specific? What do you mean by...? How or why is it important?	I think it means that... In other words... It's important because... It's similar to when...
Support Ideas with Evidence	Can you give any examples from the text? What are some examples from other texts? What evidence do you see for that? How can you justify that idea? Can you show me where the text says that?	The text says that... An example from another text is... According to... Some evidence that supports that is...
Build On or Challenge Partner's Ideas	What do you think of the idea that...? Can we add to this idea? Do you agree? What are other ideas/points of view? What else do we need to think about? How does that connect to the idea...?	I would add that... I want to follow up on your idea... Another way to look at it is... What you said made me think of...
Paraphrase	What do we know so far? To recap, I think that... I'm not sure that was clear. How can we relate what I said to the topic/question?	So, you are saying that... Let me see if I understand you... Do you mean that...? In other words... It sounds like you are saying that...
Determine the Main Idea and Key Details	What have we discussed so far? How can we summarize what we have talked about? What can we agree upon? What are main points or ideas we can share? What relevant details support the main points or ideas? What key ideas can we take away?	We can say that... The main idea seems to be... As a result of this conversation, we think that we should... The evidence suggests that...

Strategies for Classroom Discussion

Providing multiple opportunities to speak in the classroom and welcoming all levels of participation will motivate English learners to take part in class discussions and build oral proficiency. These basic teaching strategies will encourage whole class and small group discussions for all language proficiency levels of English learners.

 ## Wait time/Different Response

- Be sure to give students enough time to answer the question. They may need more time to process their ideas.

- Let them know that they can respond in different ways depending on their levels of proficiency. Students can:

  - Answer in their native language; then you can rephrase in English

  - Ask a more proficient ELL speaker to repeat the answer in English

  - Answer with nonverbal cues.

 ## Elaborate

- If students give a one-word answer or a nonverbal clue, elaborate on the answer to model fluent speaking and grammatical patterns.

- Provide more examples or repeat the answer using proper academic language.

 ## Elicit

- Prompt students to give a more comprehensive response by asking additional questions or guiding them to get an answer, such as can you tell me more?

- This strategy is very effective when students are asked to justify or explain their reasoning.

Asking about Meaning

- Repeating an answer offers an opportunity to clarify the meaning of a response.

- Repeating an answer allows you to model the proper form for a response. You can model how to answer in full sentences and use academic language.

- When you repeat the answer, correct any grammar or pronunciation errors.

ENTERING/EMERGING

- What is _____?

- What does _____ mean?

- _____ is _____.

- _____ means _____.

DEVELOPING/EXPANDING

- Could you tell me what _____ means?

- _____ is similar to _____.

- _____ is another way of saying _____.

BRIDGING

- Could you give me a definition of _____?

- Can you point to the evidence from the text?

- What is the best answer? Why?

Talk about Level of Understanding

ENTERING/EMERGING	• I understand./I got it. • I don't understand this word/sentence.
DEVELOPING/EXPANDING	• Could you tell me what _____ means? • _____ is another way of saying _____.
BRIDGING	• I think I understand most of it. • I'm not sure I understand this completely.

 Justify Your Reasoning

ENTERING/EMERGING	• I think _____.
DEVELOPING/EXPANDING	• My reasons are _____.
BRIDGING	• I think _____ because _____.

Agreeing with Someone's Reasoning

ENTERING/EMERGING	• I agree with your reasons or point.
DEVELOPING/EXPANDING	• I agree that _____.
BRIDGING	• I have the same reasons as _____. I think that _____.

 Disagreeing with Someone's Reasoning

ENTERING/EMERGING	• I don't agree with your reasons.
DEVELOPING/EXPANDING	• I don't agree that _____.
BRIDGING	• I can see your point. However, I think that _____.

How to Use the Teacher Edition

The suggested strategies, activities, and tips provide additional language and concept support to accelerate English learners' acquisition of academic English.

English Learner Instructional Strategy

Each English Learner Instructional Strategy can be utilized before or during regular class instruction.

Categories of the scaffolded support are:

- Vocabulary Support
- Language Structure Support
- Sensory Support
- Graphic Support
- Collaborative Support

The goal of the scaffolding strategies is to make each individual lesson more comprehensible for ELLs by providing visual, contextual and linguistic support to foster students' understanding of basic communication in an academic context.

English Learner Instructional Strategy

Vocabulary Support: Frontload Academic Vocabulary

Write the word *reciprocal* and the Spanish cognate, *recíproco,* on the board. Then write $\frac{2}{3} \times \frac{3}{2} = ?$ Ask students to solve. *What is the answer?* **1** Repeat with another example. Explain that *reciprocals* are any two numbers with a product of one. Check students' understanding by giving examples and non-examples of reciprocals. Write *reciprocals* and a math example on the Word Wall.

Give each student the 2 through 10 cards from a set of number cards. Have one student use two cards to create a fraction. A partner must use his or her cards to create the reciprocal of that fraction. Switch roles and repeat several times.

Since ELLs benefit from visual references to new vocabulary, many of the English Learner Instruction Strategies suggest putting vocabulary words on a Word Wall. Choose a location in your classroom for your Word Wall, and organize the words by module, by topic, or alphabetically.

English Language Development Leveled Activities

These activities are tiered for Entering/Emerging, Developing/Expanding, and Bridging leveled ELLs. Activity suggestions are specific to the content of the lesson. Some activities include instruction to support students with lesson specific vocabulary that they will need to understand the math content in English, while other activities teach the concept or skill using scaffolded approaches specific to ELLs. The activities are intended for small group instruction, and can be directed by the instructor, an aide, or a peer mentor.

English Language Development Leveled Activities

Entering/Emerging	Developing/Expanding	Bridging
Word Knowledge	**Word Knowledge**	**Language Structure**
Give each pair of students 16 counters. Say, *Make three equal groups.* Monitor as partners work. Ask, *How many counters did you start with?* **16** *How many groups?* **three** *How many counters in each group?* **five** *How many extra counters do you have?* **one** Write the problem on the board and describe and label the dividend, divisor, quotient, and remainder. Teach, model, and prompt students to say the words chorally and individually. Repeat with several more problems.	Write 42 ÷ 3 = 14 on the board. Point to the equation as you prompt students to say it. Have students say it chorally and individually. Point to 42 and say, *We are dividing this number into three groups; it is the* **dividend.** Prompt students to say, **The dividend is 42.** Point to the 3 and say, *We are making three groups; it is the* **divisor.** Prompt students to say, **The divisor is 3.** Point to 14 and say, *This is how many in each group; it is the quotient.* Prompt students to say, **The quotient is 14.** Repeat as needed.	On the board, write *added, subtracted, multiplied, and divided.* Assign one multiplication expression to each pair of students. Distribute an index card to each pair. Say, *As you perform your operation write sentences that describe the process using the words on the board.* Provide sentence frames such as, **First we multiplied _____. Then we subtracted _____.** and so on. Afterward, have pairs read aloud from their index cards. Be sure students are adding the /ed/ and /d/ sounds to indicate past tense.

Student talk is **boldfaced.**

Teacher talk is **italicized.**

Multicultural Teacher Tip

In some cultures, mental math is emphasized. Students may skip intermediate steps when performing algorithms such as long division. Whereas U.S. students are taught to write the numbers they will be subtracting in the process of long division, other students will make the calculations mentally and write only the results.

Multicultural Teacher Tip

These tips provide insight on academic and cultural differences that you may encounter in your classroom. While math is the universal language, some ELLs may have been shown different methods to find the answer based on their native country, while their cultural customs may influence their learning styles and behavior in the classroom.

How to Use the Student Edition

Each student page provides ELL support for vocabulary, note taking, and writing skills. These pages can be used before, during, or after classroom instruction. A corresponding page with answers is found in the teacher resources.

Word Cards

Students define each vocabulary word or phrase and write a sentence using the term in context. Space is provided for Spanish speakers to write the definition in Spanish.

A blank word card template is provided for use with non-Spanish speaking ELLs.

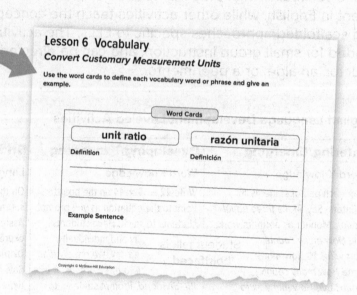

Lesson 6 Vocabulary
Convert Customary Measurement Units

Use the word cards to define each vocabulary word or phrase and give an example.

Word Cards

unit ratio	razón unitaria
Definition	Definición

Example Sentence

Vocabulary Squares

Vocabulary squares reinforce the lesson vocabulary by having students write a definition, write a sentence using the vocabulary in context, and create an example of the vocabulary. Suggest that students use translation tools and write notes in English or in their native language on the cards as well for clarification of terms. Encourage students to identify and make note of cognates to help accelerate the acquisition of math concepts in English.

Lesson 1 Vocabulary
Use Substitution to Solve One-Step Equations

Use the vocabulary squares to write a definition, a sentence, and an example for each vocabulary word.

equation	Definition
Example	Sentence

equals sign	Definition
Example	Sentence

How to Use the Student Edition continued

Three-Column Chart

Three-column charts concentrate on English/Spanish cognates. Students are given the word in English. Encourage students to use a glossary to find the word in Spanish and the definition in English. As an extension, have students identify and highlight other cognates which may be in the definitions.

A blank three-column chart template is provided for use with non-Spanish speaking ELLs.

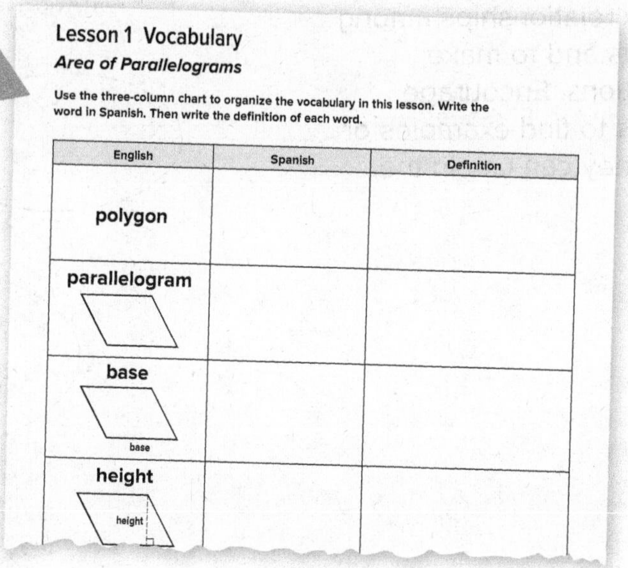

Lesson 1 Vocabulary
Area of Parallelograms

Use the three-column chart to organize the vocabulary in this lesson. Write the word in Spanish. Then write the definition of each word.

English	Spanish	Definition
polygon		
parallelogram		
base		
height		

Definition Map

The definition maps are designed to address a single vocabulary word, phrase, or concept. Students should define the word in the description box. Most definition maps will ask students to list characteristics and examples. Others, as shown at the left, will ask students to perform other tasks. Make sure you review with students the tasks required.

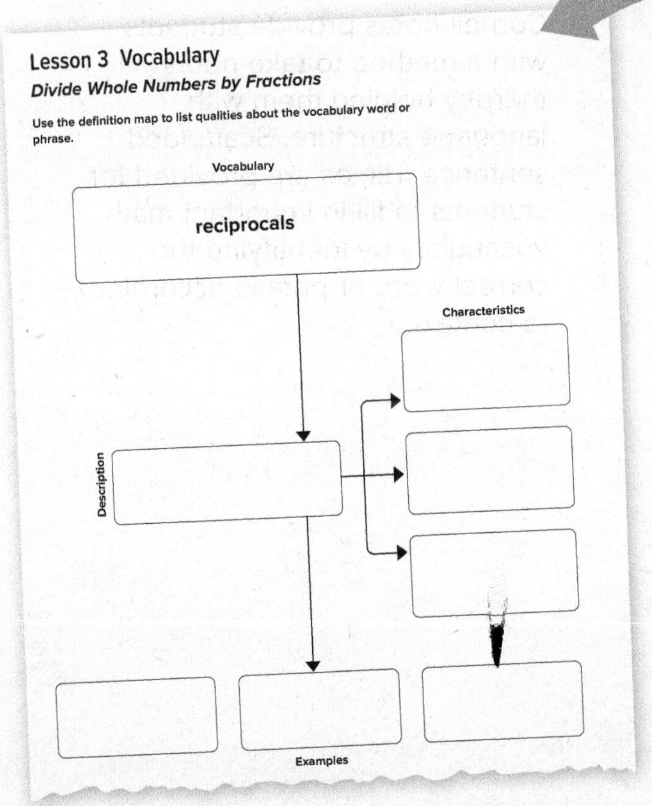

Lesson 3 Vocabulary
Divide Whole Numbers by Fractions

Use the definition map to list qualities about the vocabulary word or phrase.

Vocabulary

reciprocals

Characteristics

Description

Examples

How to Use the Student Edition *continued*

Concept Web

Concept webs are designed to show relationships among concepts and to make connections. Encourage students to find examples or words they can use in the web.

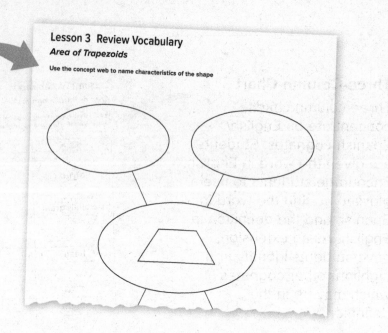

Lesson 3 Review Vocabulary
Area of Trapezoids

Use the concept web to name characteristics of the shape

Cornell Notes

Cornell notes provide students with a method to take notes thereby helping them with language structure. Scaffolded sentence frames are provided for students to fill-in important math vocabulary by identifying the correct word or phrase according to context.

Lesson 3 Notetaking
One-Step Subtraction Equations

Use Cornell notes to better understand the lesson's concepts. Complete each sentence by filling in the blanks with the correct word or phrase.

Questions	Notes
1. How can I solve a subtraction equation?	I can use _____ to solve a subtraction equation, because subtraction and _____ are _____
2. What does the Addition Property of Equality say I can do to an equation?	I can _____ the _____ number to each side of an equation and the sides will remain _____ .

English/Spanish Cognates used in Course 1

English	Spanish	VKV Page Number
absolute value	valor absoluto	VKV13
algebra	álgebra	
algebraic expression	expresión algebraica	
area	área	
Associative Property	propiedad asociative	
base	base	
coefficient	coeficiente	VKV17
Commutative Property	propiedad conmutative	VKV11
congruent	congruente	VKV23
constant	constante	
coordinate plane	plano de coordenadas	VKV3
define the variable	definir la variable	
dependent variable	variable dependiente	
distance	distancia	
distribution	distribución	
Distributive Property	propiedad distributiva	
equation	ecuación	VKV21
equivalent expressions	expresiones equivalentes	
evaluate	evaluar	VKV14
exponent	exponente	
expression	expresión	
factor the expression	factorizar la expresión	
factors	factores	
formula	fórmula	
graph	gráfica	
histogram	histograma	VKV35
Identity Property	propiedad de identidad	
independent variable	variable Independiente	
interquartile range	trango intercuartil	

English	Spanish	VKV Page Number
inverse operations	operaciones inversas	VKV21
measures of center	medidas del centro	
measures of variation	medidas de varisción	
median	mediana	VKV31
numerical expression	expresión numérica	VKV20
opposites	opuestos	VKV15
ordered pair	par ordenado	VKV5
origin	origen	VKV5
parallelogram	paralelogramo	VKV25
percent	por ciento	
polygon	polígono	VKV23
properties	propiesades	
proportion	proportión	
pyramid	pirámide	
quadrants	cuadrantes	VKV15
quartile	cuartil	VKV33
range	rango	VKV31
rational number	número racional	VKV9
reciprocal	recíproco	VKV11
rectangular prism	prisma rectangular	VKV30
solution	solución	VKV21
surface area	área de superficie	VKV27
symmetric	simétrico	VKV35
term	término	VKV19
three-dimensional figure	figura tridimensional	VKV27
triangular prism	prisma triangular	VKV29
unit price	precio unitario	VKV5
variable	variable	
vertex	vértice	
volume	volumen	
x-coordinate	coordenada x	VKV8
y-coordinate	coordenada y	VKV7

NAME _____ DATE _____ PERIOD _____

Lesson _____

Use the word cards to define each vocabulary word or phrase and give an example.

Word Cards

_____   _____

Definition

_____   _____

_____   _____

_____   _____

Example Sentence

_____

_____

Copyright © McGraw-Hill Education

- -

Word Cards

_____   _____

Definition

_____   _____

_____   _____

_____   _____

Example Sentence

_____

_____

Copyright © McGraw-Hill Education

xx

Lesson _____

Use the three-column chart to organize the vocabulary in this lesson.

English	Native Language	Definition

Lesson 1 Understand Ratios

English Learner Instructional Strategy

Language Structure Support: Tiered Questions

As you work through the lesson, be sure to check students' understanding during every step. You can do this by asking questions that are appropriate to their level of English acquisition. Entering/Emerging students can point or say **yes/no**. Your instructions must be very short and clear with known vocabulary. Developing/Expanding students can give short answers and may attempt simple sentences. Bridging students can create longer sentences and synthesize more information in English.

Entering/Emerging: *Point to the correct ratio. Is this the correct ratio?*

Developing/Expanding: *What is the correct ratio?* Have students write it.

Bridging: *Explain the ratio of _____ to _____.* **The ratio of _____ to _____ is _____.** Have students write their answer as a complete sentence.

Add *ratio* to the Word Wall with a math example or picture.

English Language Development Leveled Activities

Entering/Emerging	Developing/Expanding	Bridging
Choral Responses	**Listen and Identify**	**Pairwork**
Model an example of a simple ratio from the lesson, or use your own, such as one eraser for every two pencils. Write, 1:2 on the board. Point to the expression and say, *This is a ratio.* Prompt students to say, **ratio.** Repeat chorally and then individually. Make sure students pronounce /sh/ (and not /t/) in the middle of the word. Repeat for other examples, including other ways of saying the ratio, such as *one eraser for every two pencils.* As students' language ability allows, prompt and practice the sentence **This is/isn't a ratio.**	Give each student 10 pattern blocks: four squares, three trapezoids, one rectangle, and two hexagons. Then ask them to show and write the ratios of the sets as you call them. For example, say, *Show me four squares to two trapezoids. Write the ratio.* Ask students to find the ratio of hexagons to squares expressed in three different ways: as a fraction, using a colon, and in words. Say, *Write the ratio as a fraction, with a colon, in words.*	Have partners work together. Give each pair a write-on/wipe-off board and a board marker. One partner should say a ratio, and the other partner should show it using manipulatives or by drawing on their board. For example, the first student says, **Show me a ratio of 3 pencils to 2 erasers.** The second student should use pencils and erasers to show the ratio and then write **3:2, $\frac{3}{2}$,** or **3 pencils for every 2 erasers.** Have students switch roles and repeat.

Teacher Notes:

NAME _____ DATE _____ PERIOD _____

Lesson 1 Vocabulary
Understand Ratios

Use the concept web to show the ratio of 2 to 3 in different ways. Use a
diagram in one of the pieces of the web. Sample answers are given.

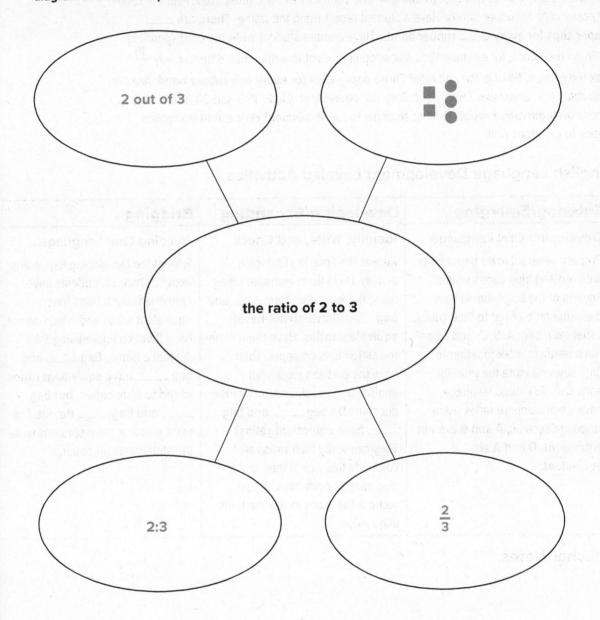

Lesson 2 Tables of Equivalent Ratios

English Learner Instructional Strategy

Sensory Support: Realia (Real-life objects used in teaching)

Prepare two containers, one with 15 paper clips and 5 rubber bands, and another with 30 paper clips and 10 rubber bands. Review *ratio, rate,* and *unit rate* from the Word Wall.

Organize students into two groups and give one container to each group. Say, *Find the ratio of paper clips to rubber bands.* Have a student report using the frame, **There are _____ paper clips for every _____ rubber bands.** Have another student write the corresponding ratio on the board, for example 15:5. Ask another student to write it in a different way: $\frac{15}{5}$. Ask the groups, *What is the unit rate?* **Three paper clips for every one rubber band.** *Are the unit rates the same?* **yes** *That's right. They are* **equivalent.** Circle 15:5 and 30:10 and say, *These are* **equivalent ratios.** Prompt students to say, **equivalent ratios.** Add *equivalent ratios* to the Word Wall.

English Language Development Leveled Activities

Entering/Emerging	Developing/Expanding	Bridging
Developing Oral Language Prepare several brown paper bags with red and blue cubes inside. Several of the bags should have the same ratio of red to blue cubes. Label each bag: A, B, C, and so on. Have partners work together to find, say, and write the ratio for each bag. To extend language, have them compare ratios using language such as, **A and B are not equivalent. D and A are equivalent.**	**Identify, Write, and Check** Repeat the Entering/Emerging activity. Have them compare ratios using the language, **Bag _____ and bag _____ [have/do not have] equivalent ratios.** Have them write the statements on paper. Then have the partners work with another pair to ask and answer the question, **Do bag _____ and bag _____ have equivalent ratios?** They can verify their ratios are correct in this way. If they find a discrepancy, both pairs should recheck the ratios inside the bags in question.	**Building Oral Language** Repeat the Developing/Expanding activity. Once all students have confirmed which bags have equivalent ratios and which do not, have them compare using the sentence frame, **Bag _____ and bag _____ have equivalent ratios of red to blue cubes, but bag _____ and bag _____ do not.** For extra practice, have students write the statements on paper.

Teacher Notes:

NAME _____ DATE _____ PERIOD _____

Lesson 2 Review Vocabulary
Tables of Equivalent Ratios

Use the definition map to list qualities about the vocabulary word or phrase.
Sample answers are given.

Vocabulary

equivalent ratios

**Characteristics
(What is it like?)**

have the same unit rate

Description

show the same relationship between quantities

have the same unit price

When written as fractions, the fractions are equivalent.

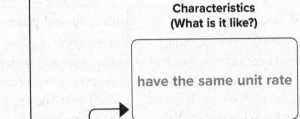

4:5 = 12:15

$\dfrac{15 \text{ feet}}{3 \text{ jumps}} = \dfrac{10 \text{ feet}}{2 \text{ jumps}}$

$\dfrac{30 \text{ songs}}{\$15} = \dfrac{15 \text{ songs}}{\$7.50}$

Examples

Lesson 3 Graphs of Equivalent Ratios
English Learner Instructional Strategy

Graphic Support: Coordinate Planes

Copy and enlarge a coordinate plane. Write *ordered pair (x-coordinate, y-coordinate)* at the bottom of the sheet. Laminate the sheet or put it in a clear pocket protector. Make enough for each pair of students. Have students use a board marker and the enlarged coordinate plane as they go through the examples.

Write the terms (and cognates, if applicable) *coordinate plane (plano de coordenadas), origin (origen), x-axis, y-axis, ordered pair (par ordenado), x-coordinate (coordenada x), y-coordinate (coordenada y),* and *graph (gráfica)* on the Word Wall with pictorial descriptions.

English Language Development Leveled Activities

Entering/Emerging	Developing/Expanding	Bridging
Word Knowledge	**Identify and Write**	**Show What You Know**
Give each student a coordinate plane with each of the following clearly visible but not labeled: origin, ordered pair, *x*-axis, *y*-axis. Point to the entire grid and say, *This is a coordinate plane.* Prompt students to say *coordinate plane.* Write it on the board, and have students write it on their papers. Repeat for *origin, ordered pair, x-axis, y-axis, x-coordinate, y-coordinate,* having students label the parts as they learn them. Check students' understanding by saying, *Put your finger on the origin. What is the x-coordinate?* and so on until students are firm.	Give pairs of students a number cube. Have one student roll numbers for the *x*-coordinate and the other roll numbers for the *y*-coordinate. After they create a list of at least six ordered pairs, have them assign a letter to each ordered pair. Then have the partners create a coordinate plane and graph the ordered pairs. Encourage them to use language such as: **The *x*-coordinate is _____ . The *y*-coordinate is _____ . The ordered pair is _____ .**	Give each student a piece of graph paper. Have them draw a coordinate plane with axes numbered to 10. Then have them draw a figure with at least four vertices positioned at different coordinates. For example, the figure could be a square with vertices at (0, 0), (0, 5), (5, 5), and (5, 0). After drawing their figures and noting the coordinates, have them dictate their drawing to a partner who should plot the points and connect the dots with lines to create the same shape. Have them compare drawings. Are they the same?

Teacher Notes:

NAME _____ DATE _____ PERIOD _____

Lesson 3 Vocabulary

Graphs of Equivalent Ratios

Use the concept web to identify the parts of the coordinate plane. Use the words from the word bank.

Word Bank		
origin	x-axis	y-axis
ordered pair	x-coordinate	y-coordinate

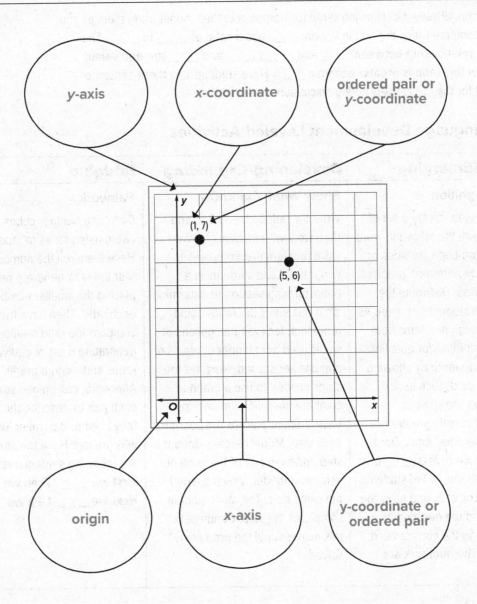

Lesson 4 Compare Ratio Relationships

English Learner Instructional Strategy

Vocabulary Support: Utilize Resources

As students review and utilize previously taught vocabulary, such as *ratio, equivalent ratios, ordered pairs, coordinate plane,* and *ratio table,* be sure to remind them that they can refer to their math glossaries for help. Direct students to other translation tools as well if they are having difficulty with nonmath language in the problems, such as *protein, pepperonis, sunflower seeds, peanuts, cereal,* and so on. You may also consider replacing less-familiar terms with vocabulary that may be more familiar, such as *running* and *swimming* instead of *cardio* and *resistance.*

Before the lesson, display the following sentence frames, and then model using them as you describe and compare ratios during the lesson: **_____ has a ratio of _____ to _____. The ratio shows a relationship between _____ and _____. _____ and _____ are equivalent rations. I know this ratio is greater because _____.** Have students use these sentence frames as well for their responses during discussions.

English Language Development Leveled Activities

Entering/Emerging	Developing/Expanding	Bridging
Word Recognition	**Show What You Know**	**Pairwork**
Before the lesson, create a set of index cards with the following word pairs written on opposite sides of the cards: *same/different, greater/ lesser, more/less.* Distribute the cards so each student has a set. As you work through problems from the lesson, ask either/or questions that can be answered by showing one side of a card, such as *Are these numbers the same or different? Is this ratio greater or lesser than the other ratio? Does _____ have more or less _____ than _____?* Choose one of the students who answer correctly and have the student reword the question as a statement using the correct word, for example, **The numbers are different.**	Write the ratios 1:5 and 2:4, and then work with students to write a word problem that compares the two ratios. Lead students in a brainstorming session to determine what quantities the ratios could represent, for example, gallons of water used per number of plants or pull-ups per second. Next, list the steps needed to use a graph to compare the ratio relationships. Invite student pairs to the board for each step. Model reading aloud the step and have one of the students echo your model, reading aloud the same step. The other student completes the step. Continue in this manner until the problem is solved.	Distribute number cubes and blank coordinate planes to student pairs. Have them roll the number cubes four times to generate two ratios, placing the smaller number first in each ratio. Then have them compare the ratio relationships by generating a set of equivalent ratios and using a graph. Afterward, call on one student from each pair to describe the process they used to determine which ratio was greater. Have the student use the following sentence starters: **First we _____. Then we _____. Next we _____. Last we _____.**

Teacher Notes:

NAME _____ DATE _____ PERIOD _____

Lesson 4 Notetaking
Compare Ratio Relationships

Use Cornell notes to better understand the lesson's concepts. Complete each sentence by filling in the blanks with the correct word or phrase.

Questions	Notes
1. How can I use a line graph to compare ratio relationships?	I can use ___scaling___ to generate ___equivalent___ ratios and use them as ___ordered pairs___ in a graph. Then I can draw a ___line___ through the points of each ratio relationship. The ___greater___ ratio will have the ___steeper___ line.
2. How can I use a table to compare ratio relationships?	I can use ___scaling___ to generate ___equivalent___ ratios. When one quantity in each relationship is ___the same___, I can ___compare___ the ratios by looking at the other quantity. The ___greater___ ratio will have the ___greater___ number.

Summary

When is it better to use a table instead of a line graph to compare ratio relationships? **See students work.**

_____
_____
_____
_____
_____
_____

Lesson 5 Solve Ratio Problems

English Learner Instructional Strategy

Language Structure Support: Tiered Questions

As you work through the lesson, be sure to check ELL students' understanding during every step. You can do this by asking questions that are appropriate to their level of English acquisition. Entering/Emerging students can point or say **yes/no**. Your instructions must be very short and clear with known vocabulary. Developing/Expanding students can give short answers and may attempt simple sentences. Bridging students can create longer sentences and synthesize more information in English.

Entering/Emerging students: Point to the correct ratio. *Is this the correct ratio?*

Developing/Expanding students: *What is the correct ratio?* Have students write it.

Bridging students: *Explain the ratio of _____ to _____.* **The ratio of _____ to _____ is _____.** Have students write their answer as a complete sentence.

Add *ratio* to the Math Word Wall with a math example or picture.

English Language Development Leveled Activities

Entering/Emerging	Developing/Expanding	Bridging
Choral Responses	**Listen and Identify**	**Pairwork**
Model an example of a simple ratio from the lesson. Or use your own, such as one eraser for every two pencils. Write *1:2* on the board. Point to the expression and say, *This is a ratio.* Prompt students to say, **ratio**. Repeat chorally and then individually. Make sure students pronounce /sh/ (and not /t/) in the middle of the word. Repeat for other examples, including other ways of saying the ratio, such as *one eraser for every two pencils.* As students' language ability allows, prompt and practice the sentence **This is/isn't a ratio.**	Give each student 10 pattern blocks: four squares, three trapezoids, one rectangle, and two hexagons. (Other items, such as paper clips and pencils may be used.) Then ask them to show and write the ratios of the sets as you call them. For example, say, *Show me four squares to two trapezoids. Write the ratio.* Ask students to find the ratio of hexagons to squares expressed in three different ways: as a fraction, using a colon, and in words. Say, *Write the ratio as a fraction/with a colon/in words.*	Have partners work together. Give each pair a write-on/wipe-off board and a board marker. One partner should say a ratio, and the other partner should show it using manipulatives or by drawing on their board. For example, the first student says, **Show me a ratio of 3 pencils to 2 erasers**. The second student should use pencils and erasers to show the ratio and then write **3:2**, $\frac{3}{2}$, or **3 pencils for every 2 erasers**. Have students switch roles and repeat.

Teacher Notes:

NAME _____ DATE _____ PERIOD _____

Lesson 5 Review Vocabulary

Solve Ratio Problems

Use the vocabulary squares to write a definition, a sentence, and an example for each vocabulary word.

	Definition
ratio	a comparison of two quantities by division
Example	**Sentence**
$\frac{3}{5}$, 3:5, 3 to 5, 3 out of 5	There are 3 pencils and 5 pens. 3:5 is the ratio of pencils to pens.

	Definition
equivalent ratios	two ratios that express the same relationship between quantities; equivalent fractions
Example	**Sentence**
$\frac{4}{5}$ and $\frac{120}{150}$	9 out of 10 dentists recommend *Sparkle* toothpaste to their patients. So, in a group of 200 dentists, there will be 180 who recommend *Sparkle* toothpaste.

Lesson 6 Convert Customary Measurement Units

English Learner Instructional Strategy

Vocabulary Support: Sentence Frames

Write the terms *unit ratio* and *convert* and their Spanish cognates, *razón unitaria* and *convertir*, on the board. Show students a 12-inch ruler. Say, *This is one foot. How many inches per foot?* **12** Write $\frac{12 \text{ in.}}{1 \text{ ft}}$ on the board. Point to the 1 in the denominator and say, *When the denominator is 1, it is a unit ratio.* Prompt students to say, **unit ratio**.

Write several conversion problems on the board. Make sure to include conversions involving yards and feet, pints and cups, quarts and gallons, and so on. Assign one problem to each pair. Display the following sentence frames to help students share how they found their solution:

To convert _____ to _____, I multiplied/divided by _____.

The remainder is _____, so there are _____ left over.

English Language Development Leveled Activities

Entering/Emerging	Developing/Expanding	Bridging
Word Recognition and Phonemic Awareness length, weight, and capacity units: foot, yard, mile, pound, ton, cup, pint, quart, gallon. As you introduce each word, model clear pronunciation, and prompt students to repeat. Help students report about unit ratios using the sentence frame, **There are [number][unit] in [number][unit].**	**Recognize and Act It Out** Review unit conversion ratios. Have students make "human unit ratios." Use masking tape to create a large fraction bar on the floor; put a 1 in the denominator. Say, for example, *Show me the ratio of cups to pints.* Have the appropriate number of students create the numerator in the cups-to-pints unit ratio. There should be 2 students in the "numerator."	**Building Oral Language** Have partners give each other conversion problems and solve them. Preteach different ways of presenting a problem: **Convert _____ to _____. How do you convert _____ to _____? What is the conversion of _____ to _____? How many _____ are in _____?** Encourage partners to answer in complete sentences and to explain their process for solving: **There are [number][unit] in [number][unit]. I can convert _____ to _____ by multiplying/dividing _____. The answer is _____.**

Multicultural Teacher Tip

As the metric system is the standard throughout most parts of the world, ELLs will likely be more familiar with units of metric measurement than they will be with standard units. Students who have worked only with the metric system in the past will be more experienced with partial amounts written as decimals, not fractions.

NAME _____ DATE _____ PERIOD _____

Lesson 6 Vocabulary
Convert Customary Measurement Units

Use the word cards to define each vocabulary word or phrase and give an example. Sample answers are given.

Word Cards

unit ratio	razón unitaria
Definition	**Definición**
a rate where the denominator	tasa unitaria en que el
is one unit	denominador es la unidad

Example Sentence

Sample answer: The unit rate was 3 cars per hour, or $\frac{3 \text{ cars}}{1 \text{ hour}}$.

Word Cards

customary system	sistema usual
Definition	**Definición**
The units of measurement	Conjunto de unidades de
most often used in the United	medida de uso más frecuente
States.	en Estados Unidos.

Example Sentence

Sample answer: The customary system measurement for

distance is miles, which can be converted to kilometers.

Lesson 7 Understand Rates and Unit Rates
English Learner Instructional Strategy

Vocabulary Support: Check Concepts

Check students' understanding of the vocabulary that they have been learning. Write the following example on the board: *Sam picked 45 oranges in 5 minutes. Write this rate as a unit rate.* Work through the example. Ask the following questions and write the answers on the board, *What was the **unit**?* **oranges** *At what **rate** did she pick the oranges?* **45 oranges in 5 minutes**. *What was the **unit rate**?* **9 oranges in 1 minute**. Try to tier questions similar to the following:

Entering/Emerging: *Point to the rate.*

Developing/Expanding: *What is the rate?* **45 oranges in 5 minutes**.

Bridging: *How do you find a unit rate?* **Divide the number of oranges by the number of minutes**.

Add *rate* and *unit rate* to the Word Wall with examples.

English Language Development Leveled Activities

Entering/Emerging	Developing/Expanding	Bridging
Word Knowledge	**Word Knowledge**	**Look and Identify**
Give each student a photo of a different item. Point to one of the photos and ask, *What is the price for one _____?* Elicit a price—for example, $2—and have all students say in unison: **Two dollars for one _____**. Write $\frac{\$2}{1 \text{ (item name)}}$ on the board. Point to the ratio and say, *This is a **unit price**.* Prompt students to say, **unit price**. Then say, *A unit price is the price for **one** item.* Ask, *A unit price is the price of how many items?* **one** Repeat the activity for the other students' photos.	Set a timer, and see how many times a student can hop on one foot in one minute. Write the student's result on the board. For example, if Carla jumped 75 times in one minute, write Carla: $\frac{75 \text{ jumps}}{1 \text{ minute}}$. Point to the ratio and say, *This is a **unit rate**.* Prompt students to say, **unit rate**. Have all students time themselves to find the unit rate for hopping on one foot.	Write several examples of rates and unit rates on index cards and put them in a box. Have one student draw a card from the box and hold it up so that the group can see it. Students should identify the ratio as either a rate or a unit rate, and explain how they made their determination. Have students take turns drawing cards.

Multicultural Teacher Tip

Many cultures emphasize the use of decimal numbers over fractions. For this reason, ELLs may be unfamiliar with fractions and how they describe the relationship between a part and the whole. You may want to create a chart showing common fractions, their decimal equivalents, and a visual example, such as a shaded circle or rectangle.

NAME _____ DATE _____ PERIOD _____

Lesson 7 Vocabulary
Understand Rates and Unit Rates

Use the vocabulary squares to write a definition, a sentence, and an example for each vocabulary word. Sample answers are given.

	Definition
unit price	the cost per unit
Example	**Sentence**
$1.25 per pound	I bought three pounds of apples for $3.75. The unit price was $1.25 per pound.

	Definition
rate	a ratio comparing two quantities of different kinds of units
Example	**Sentence**
$\dfrac{100 \text{ words}}{5 \text{ minutes}}$	I can type 100 words in 5 minutes. I can type at a rate of $\dfrac{100 \text{ words}}{5 \text{ minutes}}$.

	Definition
unit rate	a rate that is simplified so the denominator is 1
Example	**Sentence**
$\dfrac{20 \text{ words}}{1 \text{ minute}}$	I can type 100 words in 5 minutes. I can type at a unit rate of $\dfrac{20 \text{ words}}{1 \text{ minute}}$ or 20 words per minute.

Lesson 8 Solve Rate Problems

English Learner Instructional Strategy

Collaborative Support: Echo Reading

As students encounter word problems, have partners echo read. One partner reads the problem, and then the other partner reads it. (If the problem is more than one sentence, partners can echo read one sentence at a time.) After reading each problem, students should underline the key words or write them on paper. Then have them compare the key words they identified. If a student does not understand a word, they should ask their partner, **What does _____ mean?** If neither partner knows, they may ask you.

Encourage students to ask and answer the questions, **What do we need to find? What do we know? What is the rate? What is the unit rate/price?** Have partners work together and ask and answer the questions as they complete each Exercise.

English Language Development Leveled Activities

Use the following problem with these leveled activities:

Lucas is putting floor tile on his kitchen floor. He bought six boxes of floor tile for $78. He needs another four boxes of tile. How much will Lucas pay for the four boxes of tile?

Entering/Emerging	Developing/Expanding	Bridging
Look and Identify	**Look and Identify**	**Public Speaking Norms**
Write the problem on the board and read it with students. Point out "six boxes for $78." Ask *How can you write this as a ratio?* $\frac{\$78}{6 \text{ boxes}}$ *Is this a rate?* **yes** *Is this a unit rate?* **no** Encourage students to use complete sentences to describe the rate or unit rate such as, **The rate is 6 boxes per $78.** or **The unit rate is $13 per box.**	Review the different ways a rate can be written: as a fraction, with a colon, or in words. Have partners work together to identify the rates in the problem. Encourage students to use the language, **I think the rate is _____. I think the unit rate is _____.**	Have students do a role-play to explain how they found the unit rate for the problem. Suggest they use a question-and-answer model: Student 1: **How did you find the answer to the problem?** Student 2: **First, I found the rate for the floor tile. The rate is $78 for 6 boxes.** Student 1: **And then what did you do?** Student 2: **I found the answer by using equivalent fractions. I know that the unit rate is $\frac{\$13}{1 \text{ box}}$. I know an equivalent rate is $\frac{\$52}{4 \text{ boxes}}$, so Lucas spent $52 on four more boxes of floor tiles.** Make sure students use a gerund (*-ing* form) after the prepostion *by*. Switch roles and repeat the activity using another example problem.

NAME _____ DATE _____ PERIOD _____

Lesson 8 Review Vocabulary

Solve Rate Problems

Complete the four-square chart to review the multiple-meaning word.
Sample answers are given.

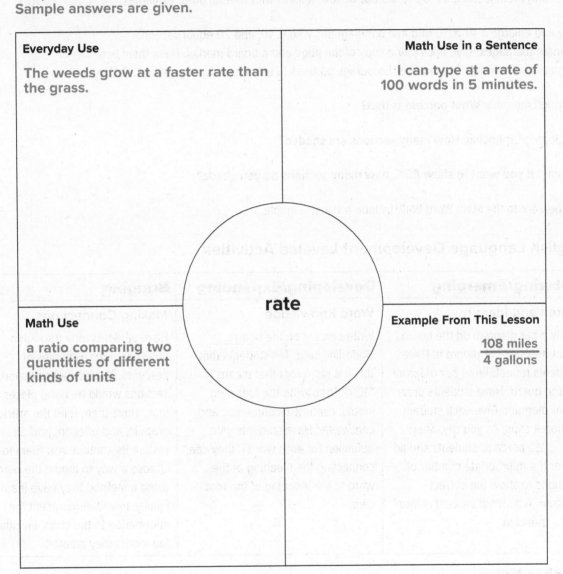

Everyday Use

The weeds grow at a faster rate than the grass.

Math Use in a Sentence

I can type at a rate of 100 words in 5 minutes.

rate

Math Use

a ratio comparing two quantities of different kinds of units

Example From This Lesson

$\dfrac{108 \text{ miles}}{4 \text{ gallons}}$

Read the sentence. Then answer the questions below.

A car can drive 108 miles with 4 gallons of gasoline.

1. What is the rate? $\dfrac{108 \text{ miles}}{4 \text{ gallons}}$

2. What is the unit rate? $\dfrac{27 \text{ miles}}{1 \text{ gallon}}$

8 Course 1 · Module 1 *Ratios and Rates*

Lesson 1 Understand Percents

English Learner Instructional Strategies

Graphic Support: Grids and Bar Diagrams

Write *percent* and its Spanish cognate, *por ciento,* on the board or a cognate chart. Explain that *percent* means "for every 100" or "out of 100." Ask, *So, what is 20 percent?* If necessary, model and prompt students to say, **20 out of 100**. Repeat with several other examples.

Copy and enlarge a 10 × 10 grid and bar diagrams with 4, 10, and 20 equal sections. Laminate the pages. Give each pair a copy of the page and a board marker. Have them use the graphics to model the examples. Encourage partners to ask and answer questions, such as:

Entering/Emerging: **What percent is that?**

Developing/Expanding: **How many sections are shaded?**

Bridging: **If you want to show 45%, how many sections do you shade?**

Add *percent* to the Math Word Wall. Include a visual example.

English Language Development Leveled Activities

Entering/Emerging	Developing/Expanding	Bridging
Listen and Identify Draw a bar diagram on the board. Point and say, *bar diagram.* Have students repeat. Write *bar diagram* on the board. Have students draw a bar diagram. Give each student 10 paper clips. As you say, *Show me _____ percent,* students should cover the appropriate number of sections to show the correct percent. Ask, *What percent is that?* **_____ percent**	**Word Knowledge** Write *percent* on the board. Underline *cent.* Tell students that this is a word root that means "100." Then write the following words: *century, bicentennial,* and *centimeter.* Have students give definition for each word if they can, connecting the meaning of the word to the meaning of the root *cent.*	**Making Connections** Have students look through a newspaper for examples of percents. The business or sports sections would be good places to look. Have them read the article or graphic, and offer support as they restate its content. Ask them to choose a way to model the percent using a method they have learned. Finally, have them present the information to the class, including the model they created.

Teacher Notes:

NAME _____ DATE _____ PERIOD _____

Lesson 1 Vocabulary
Understand Percents

Draw a line to connect *50 percent* to each correct equivalent example.

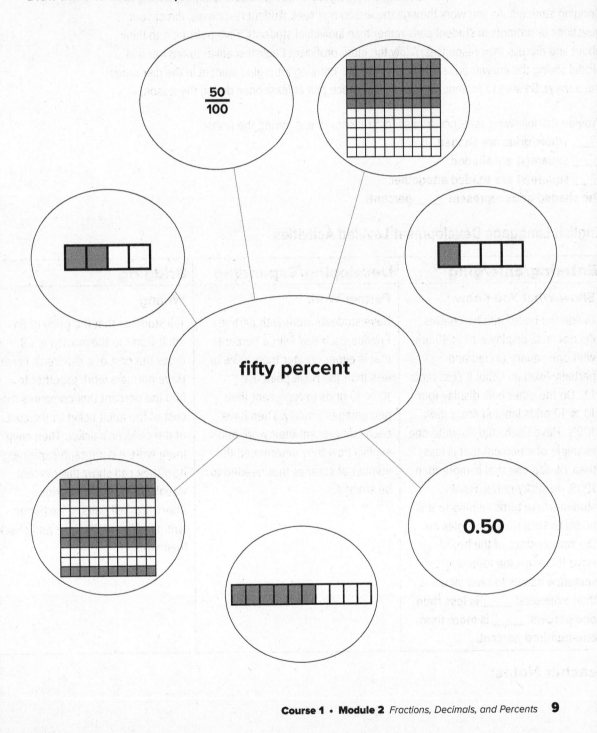

Lesson 2 Percents Greater Than 100% and Less Than 1%

English Learner Instructional Strategy

Collaborative Support: Think-Pair-Share

Before beginning the lesson, pair Entering/Emerging students with Developing/Expanding or Bridging students. As you work through the lesson and seek student responses, direct your questions or prompts to student pairs rather than individual students. Give pairs time to think about and discuss their responses. Allow the more proficient English speaker to answer first. Model saying the answer again, and then have the Entering/Emerging student in the pair repeat the answer. Be sure to prompt a response from each pair at least once during the lesson.

Provide the following sentence frames for students to use during the lesson:

_____ **whole grids are shaded.**

_____ **square(s) are shaded.**

_____ **square(s) are shaded altogether.**

The shaded grids represent _____ percent.

English Language Development Leveled Activities

Entering/Emerging	Developing/Expanding	Bridging
Show What You Know	**Partner Work**	**Writing**
Divide the board into two halves. On one half, display a 10 × 10 grid with one square circled and partially filled in. Label it *Less than 1%*. On the other half, display four 10 × 10 grids labeled *More than 100%*. Have each student write one example of a percent that is less than 1% and one that is more than 100% on sticky notes. Have students take turns coming to the board to stick their examples on the correct sides of the board. Have them use the following sentence frames to read aloud their examples: _____ **is less than one percent.** _____ **is more than one-hundred percent.**	Have students work with partners. Provide each pair with a percent that is either greater than 100% or less than 1%. Have pairs use 10 × 10 grids to represent their percentages visually. Then have each pair present their work and explain how they determined the number of squares that needed to be shaded.	Tell students that the price of an adult ticket to the movies is 1.8 times the cost of a children's ticket. Have partners work together to find the percent that compares the cost of the adult ticket to the cost of the children's ticket. Then have them write a paragraph explaining how they can show this percent visually using 10 × 10 grids. Afterward, tell pairs to exchange writing with another pair and check their work.

Teacher Notes:

NAME _____ DATE _____ PERIOD _____

Lesson 2 Vocabulary
Percents Greater Than 100% and Less Than 1%

Use words from the word bank to fill in the boxes and blanks. Some words will be used more than once.

Word Bank				
percent	less than	part	whole	greater than

$$\overset{\times 50}{\frown}$$

part $\longrightarrow$ $\dfrac{3}{2} = \dfrac{150}{100}$ } $\longleftarrow$ percent

whole $\longrightarrow$

$$\underset{\times 50}{\smile}$$

Percents are more than 100% when the number being compared to 100 is ____greater than____ 100.

$$\overset{\times 2.5}{\frown}$$

part $\longrightarrow$ $\dfrac{0.05}{40} = \dfrac{0.125}{100}$ } $\longleftarrow$ percent

whole $\longrightarrow$

$$\underset{\times 2.5}{\smile}$$

Percents are less than 1% when the number being compared to 100 is ____less than____ one.

Lesson 3 Relate Fractions, Decimals, and Percents

English Learner Instructional Strategy

Language Structure: Support Modeled Talk

Check students' pronunciation of the decimals and fractions they are working with, particularly those ending in /ths/. The *th* sound can be very difficult for many ELLs. To illustrate the pronunciation of /th/, demonstrate proper tongue placement between your teeth. Then hold a piece of paper in front of your mouth as you blow out through your teeth, saying /thththth/. Have students practice. Then review the pronunciation of *tenths, hundredths,* and *thousandths.* Say each word in isolation, and have students repeat chorally at first and then individually.

Encourage students to use the following language when they need help or clarification during the lesson:

Entering/Emerging: **Is this correct? I don't understand.**

Developing/Expanding: **Is this the correct answer? I don't understand how to solve this problem.**

Bridging: **Could you please help me with this problem? I understand _____, but _____ does not make sense.**

English Language Development Leveled Activities

Entering/Emerging	Developing/Expanding	Bridging
Listen, Say, and Write	**Word Knowledge**	**Numbered Heads Together**
Give each student a laminated 10 × 10 grid and marker. Hold up the grid and ask, *How many squares?* 100 Say, *Show me 25 percent.* Monitor as students shade in 25 squares on the grid. Say, *Yes, 25% is 25 out of 100.* Prompt students to say, 25 out of 100. Have students write *25%* and *25 out of 100* on their grids. Then model another way to write *25 out of 100:* $\frac{25}{100}$. Point to the fraction and say, *twenty-five hundredths.* Prompt students to say, **twenty-five hundredths.** Then have them write the fraction on the grid. Repeat for other percents.	Prepare a set of matching index cards consisting of fractions, decimals, and percents of equal value. For example, 25%, $\frac{1}{4}$, and 0.25. Create enough sets so each student will receive one card. Prior to the activity, review the vocabulary: *fraction, numerator, denominator, decimal, decimal point, percent.* Distribute the cards randomly to students, and have them work together to match values and form groups of three. Have groups use the reviewed vocabulary to describe the numbers on their cards and how they know the values are equivalent.	Organize students into groups of four and assign a number 1 to 4 to each student. Have the small groups work together as they solve one of the Apply problems from the lesson. They should discuss the problem, agree on a solution, and ensure that everyone in the group understands and can give the answer. When it is time to review the answer, call out a random number from 1 to 4. The students assigned to that number should raise their hands, and when called on, will answer for the team using a sentence frame: **The fraction of _____ is _____.**

Teacher Notes:

NAME _____ DATE _____ PERIOD _____

Lesson 3 Notetaking

Relate Fractions, Decimals, and Percents

Use Cornell notes to better understand the lesson's concepts. Complete each sentence by filling in the blanks with the correct word or phrase.

Questions	Notes
1. How do I write a fraction as a percent?	Find an ____equivalent____ ratio with ____100____ as the denominator. Write the ____numerator____ by itself followed by a ____% sign____ to show the percent.
2. How do I write a decimal as a percent?	First, write the decimal as a ____fraction____. The ____denominator____ will be equal to the place value of the last ____nonzero____ digit. Then find an ____equivalent____ ratio with ____100____ as the denominator. Write the ____numerator____ by itself followed by a ____% sign____ to show the percent.
3. How do I write a percent as a decimal?	Divide by ____100____ and remove the ____% sign____. This is the same as moving the decimal point ____two____ places to the ____left____.

Summary

What is the relationship between fractions, decimals, and percents?
See students' work.
_____
_____
_____
_____

Lesson 4 Find the Percent of a Number

English Learner Instructional Strategy

Sensory Support: Magazines and Newspapers

Show a store ad from a newspaper. Write *on sale at 40% off* on the board. Explain that *for sale* means that something is being sold and *on sale* means that it has a special price; *40% off* means to subtract 40% from the regular price. The amount we subtract from the regular price is the discount. The new price is the sale price.

Write an example on the board with these sale prices: DVDs: 10% off $18; CDs: 15% off $14; Games: 5% off $12. Divide students into groups. Have students determine the least expensive item. Ask emerging students to write the sale prices for each item. Have expanding students write the regular price, the discount, and the sale price for each item. Bridging students should write the steps for figuring out a sale price. Encourage students to bring native language newspapers and point out how discount and sale items are shown.

English Language Development Leveled Activities

Entering/Emerging	Developing/Expanding	Bridging
Choral and Individual Responses Compare percents. Write several percents on the board and prompt students to say in unison, ____% is [greater/less] than ____%. Then prompt individual students. For students reluctant to speak aloud, encourage them to write the sentence. Repeat for several different percents.	**Make Connections** Review *percent* on the Word Wall. Then write the following table on the board:	**Share What You Know** Create a table such as the following on the board:

Developing/Expanding table:

Snacks (300 students)	
Fruit	23%
Cheese	15%
Veggies	17%
Cookies	15%
Chips	18%
No snack	12%

Direct students to add all the percents together. Ask, *What is the total percent?* **100** Remind students that *percent* means "out of 100." Students can use this information to understand that 15% is also 15 out of 100 or $\frac{15}{100}$. Have students look at the table. Ask, *How many students will have cheese for a snack?* **45** Repeat for each of the other snack options.

Bridging table:

300	
30	10%
	25%
	35%
	78%

Review finding 10% of 300. Point to the answer space for 35% of 300 and ask, *Is this answer greater than or less than 30?* **Greater than 30.** Ask students to explain their answer to an entering/emerging level partner in terms they can understand. **I know because 35% is greater than 10%.** Repeat for other percents. Then repeat the process for a number other than 300.

Teacher Notes:

NAME _____ DATE _____ PERIOD _____

Lesson 4 Review Vocabulary

Find the Percent of a Number

Use the concept web to write examples of twenty-five percent. Use a diagram in
at least one part of the web. Sample answers are given.

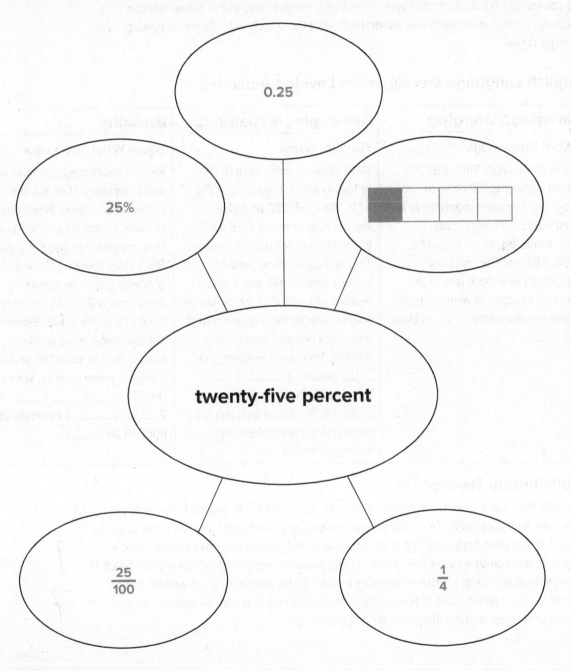

12 **Course 1 · Module 2** *Fractions, Decimals, and Percents*

Lesson 5 Estimate the Percent of a Number

English Learner Instructional Strategy

Sensory Support: Realia or Photographs

Show students a bar diagram divided in tens. Put a counter in all ten sections. Ask, *How many counters are there?* **10** Then, secretly change the number of counters on the diagram to 8, then give students a half-second peek at the diagram. Ask, *How many counters are there?* Students may have different answers, but they will probably be close. Say, *Are you sure or did you guess?* Tell students that when they find a number close to the actual number, they estimate. Prompt students to say, **estimate**. Repeat the activity with objects in photographs or other realia.

English Language Development Leveled Activities

Entering/Emerging	Developing/Expanding	Bridging
Word Knowledge Review *rounding*. Write 199. Ask, *What number is 199 close to?* **200**. Say, *Yes. You used* **rounding** *to find that number.* Prompt students to say, **rounding**. Write 23%, 47%, 76%, 397, and 518 and have students round each one to the nearest benchmark number. Have them use the frame, _____ **is close to** _____.	**Number Sense** Have students write each of the following on an index card: 23%, 47%, 76%, 199, 397, and 518. Review how to round each number to the nearest benchmark number. To play a game, have partners make a percent pile and a whole number pile with their cards. Model how to play, by turning over a card from each pile and saying each number. Then say, *I estimate that* _____ *percent of* _____ *is* _____. Have students practice saying the sentence. Then have partners take turns saying the numbers and making estimates.	**Show What You Know** Review the concepts of rounding and estimating. Then ask the following questions: *When you go shopping, what do you like to buy? How are percents used in a sale?* Tell a story about a sale: *A website is having a sale on games. Everything is 26% off. The regular price of a game is $39. Estimate the sale price.* Have students discuss how to solve the problem using language such as, **We can round** _____ **to** _____. _____ **% of $** _____ **is** _____. **I estimate the price to be** _____.

Multicultural Teacher Tip

Students from Latin American countries may write their numbers in slightly different forms than their American peers. Ones and sevens can be easily confused. Latin American ones are written with a short horizontal line at the top, and at first glance, they may appear to be a seven. To distinguish a seven from a one, a Latin American seven will include a cross-hatch at the middle of the upright. Other differences to note: Eights and fours are drawn from the bottom up. As a result, fours at times appear as nines. Nines may also be drawn with a curved descender, making them look like lowercase "g"s.

NAME _____ DATE _____ PERIOD _____

Lesson 5 Notetaking
Estimate with Percents

Use Cornell notes to better understand the lesson's concepts. Complete each
sentence by filling in the blanks with the correct word or phrase.

Questions	Notes
1. How can I estimate the percent of a number?	Round the percent to the nearest _____**benchmark percent**_____, and round the number. Write the rounded percent as a rate per 100. _____**Multiply**_____ the rate and the rounded number to find the _____**estimate**_____.
2. How can I estimate using the rate per 100?	Write the percent as a rate per 100. Round the number to the nearest _____**hundred**_____. Then _____**multiply**_____ the rate by the number of hundreds.

Summary

What is the relationship between percents and fractions? **See students' work.**

_____

_____

_____

_____

_____

_____

_____

Course 1 · Module 2 *Fractions, Decimals, and Percents* **13**

Lesson 6 Find the Whole

English Learner Instructional Strategy

Language Structure Support: Tiered Language

Prepare a survey about students' likes and dislikes; for example, favorite subjects. Have students create a chart with each subject name as a row heading and survey the entire group using the question, **What subject do you like best: English, math, or art?** They can tally the responses in column 1. Have them calculate the fraction of each response in the second column in the table, and write equivalent percents in column 3. Finally, choose various number of students that liked each subject and have studens use the percents to estimate how many students were surveyed.

Entering/Emerging: **If [number] liked [subject], then _____ students were surveyed.**

Developing/Expanding: **[number] out of _____ would like [subject].**

Bridging: **I predict that [number] out of _____ would like [subject].**

English Language Development Leveled Activities

Entering/Emerging	Developing/Expanding	Bridging
Number Sense Write several sets of equivalent numbers on index cards. For example, write 0.75, 75%, and $\frac{75}{100}$ on three separate cards. Some sets should include mixed numbers as well. First shuffle the cards and have students sort the cards into one of four piles: fractions, decimals, mixed numbers, percents. Suggest students say **This is a _____.** when they are sorting. Have partners find three cards that are equivalent and say, **_____, _____, and _____ are equivalent.**	**Number Game** Give students several sets of equivalent numbers to write on index cards. For example, write 0.75, 75%, and $\frac{75}{100}$ on three separate cards. Some sets should include mixed numbers as well. Shuffle your set of cards. Draw a card and show students. Say the number and have students repeat. Then have students search in their pile of cards to find one card that is equivalent. The first student to respond must say the name of the number in order to win a point.	**Building Oral Language** Repeat the expanding level activity. Then have students put their cards in a pile, facedown. After showing one of your cards, students turn two of their cards face up. Then they compare the cards using the following language: **[Student's 1st number] is equivalent to [teacher's number], but [student's 2nd number] is not. Both [1st number] and [2nd number] are equivalent to [teacher's number]. Neither [1st number] nor [2nd number] are equivalent to [teacher's number].**

Multicultural Teacher Tip

Because many word problems involve money, ELLs will benefit from an increased understanding of American coins and bills. A graphic organizer that visually compares coin and bill values and models how to write dollars and cents in decimal form would help. You may also want to have students describe the monetary systems of their native countries. Identifying similarities or differences with the American system can help familiarize students with dollars and cents.

NAME _____ DATE _____ PERIOD _____

Lesson 6 Vocabulary

Find the Whole

Use the concept web to find the whole. Use a double number line and equivalent ratios.

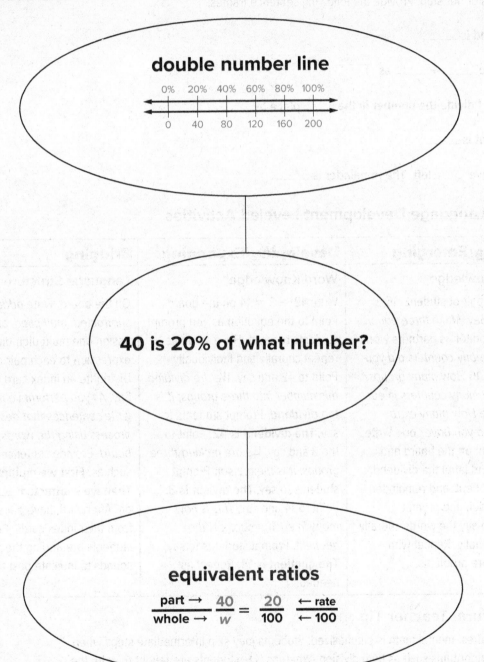

Lesson 1 Divide Multi-Digit Whole Numbers
English Learner Instructional Strategy

Collaborative Support: Round the Table

Divide students into three groups. Be sure each group contains students of varying levels of English proficiency. On the board, write $351 \div 9$. Have the students in each group take turns completing a step necessary for performing the operation. As they work, each student will describe his or her step. Provide the following sentence frames:

The dividend is _____.

First, I write _____ ÷ _____ as $)\overline{}$.

Then/Next, I divide the number in the _____ place by _____.

The quotient is _____.

Finally, I have _____ left. The remainder is _____.

English Language Development Leveled Activities

Entering/Emerging	Developing/Expanding	Bridging
Word Knowledge	**Word Knowledge**	**Language Structure**
Give each pair of students 16 counters. Say, *Make three equal groups.* Monitor as partners work. Ask, *How many counters did you start with?* **16** *How many groups?* **three** *How many counters in each group?* **five** *How many extra counters do you have?* **one** Write the problem on the board and describe and label the dividend, divisor, quotient, and remainder. Teach, model, and prompt students to say the words chorally and individually. Repeat with several more problems.	Write $42 \div 3 = 14$ on the board. Point to the equation as you prompt students to say it. Have students repeat chorally and individually. Point to 42 and say, *We are dividing this number into three groups; it is the* **dividend**. Prompt students to say, **The dividend is 42.** Point to the 3 and say, *We are making three groups; it is the* **divisor**. Prompt students to say, **The divisor is 3.** Point to 14 and say, *This is how many in each group; it is the quotient.* Prompt students to say, **The quotient is 14.** Repeat as needed.	On the board, write *added, subtracted, multiplied,* and *divided*. Assign one multi-digit division expression to each pair of students. Distribute an index card to each pair. Say, *As you perform your operation write sentences that describe the process using the words on the board.* Provide sentence frames such as, **First we multiplied _____. Then we subtracted _____.** and so on. Afterward, have pairs read aloud from their index cards. Be sure students are adding the /ed/ and /d/ sounds to indicate past tense.

Multicultural Teacher Tip

In some cultures, mental math is emphasized. Students may skip intermediate steps when performing algorithms such as long division. Whereas U.S. students are taught to write the numbers they will be subtracting in the process of long division, other students will make the calculations mentally and write only the results.

NAME _____ DATE _____ PERIOD _____

Lesson 1 Review Vocabulary
Divide Multi-Digit Whole Numbers

Use the concept web to identify the parts of a division problem. Use the terms from the word bank. Sample answers are given.

Word Bank			
dividend	divisor	quotient	remainder

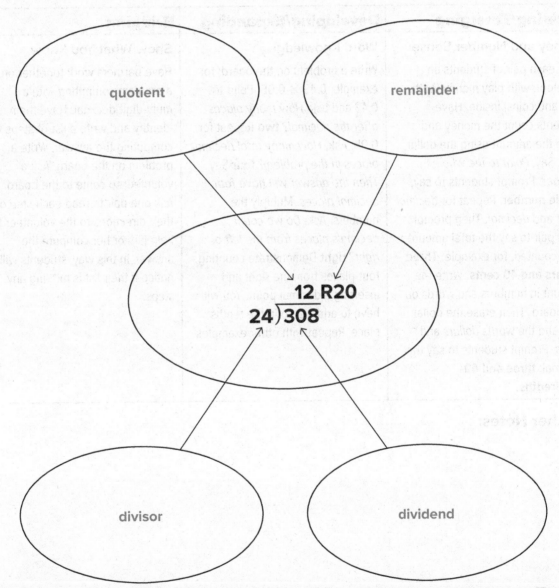

Lesson 2 Compute with Multi-Digit Decimals
English Learner Instructional Strategy

Sensory Support: Total Physical Response

Say, *Everyone, please line up.* Students should get in a straight line. Say, *This is how you line up.* Prompt students to say, **line up.** Next, show students a model of a building, made from interlocking blocks. Say, *We need more space in this building. We need to **annex** it.* Have students create another, smaller part of the building. Say, *This is an annex. I just annexed the building.* Prompt students to say, **annex.** Have students practice annexing and lining up other items.

English Language Development Leveled Activities

Entering/Emerging	Developing/Expanding	Bridging
Money and Number Sense	**Word Knowledge**	**Show What You Know**
Give each pair of students an envelope with play money (both bills and coins) inside. Have students count the money and write the amount using the dollar sign. Say, *Point to the whole number.* Prompt students to say, **whole number.** Repeat for *decimal point* and *decimal.* Then prompt each pair to say the total amount they counted, for example, **Three dollars and 49 cents.** Write the amount in numbers and words on the board. Then erase the dollar sign and the words *dollars* and *cents.* Prompt students to say the decimal: **three and 49 hundredths.**	Write a problem on the board; for example, 0.43×0.05. Point to 0.43 and ask, *How many places after the decimal?* **two** Repeat for 0.05. Ask, *How many total decimal places in the problem?* **four** Say, *Then the answer will have **four** decimal places.* Multiply the numbers. Ask, *Do we count decimals places from the left or right?* **right** Demonstrate counting four places from the right and inserting a decimal point. You will have to add a zero in the tenths place. Repeat with other examples.	Have partners work together on a problem computing with a multi-digit decimal. Have them identify and write a list of steps for computing the answer. Write a problem on the board. Ask a volunteer to come to the board. Ask one pair to read each step of their directions to the volunteer to help him or her compute the answer. In this way, students will notice if their list is missing any steps.

Teacher Notes:

NAME _____ DATE _____ PERIOD _____

Lesson 2 Notetaking
Compute with Multi-Digit Decimals

Use Cornell notes to better understand the lesson's concepts. Complete each
sentence by filling in the blanks with the correct word or phrase.

Questions	Notes
1. How do I add decimals?	To add decimals, I line up the __decimal points__. Then, I add digits that have the same __place value__.
2. How do I subtract decimals?	To subtract decimals, I line up the __decimal points__. Then, I subtract the digits that have the same __place value__. I may need to __annex__, or place zeros at the end of a decimal in order to subtract.
3. When I multiply two decimals, where do I place the decimal point in the product?	Place the decimal point the same number of places from the (left/(right)) as the __sum__ of the number of decimal places in each factor.
4. When I divide a decimal by a whole number, where do I place the decimal point in the quotient?	The decimal point in the quotient is placed directly ((above)/below) the decimal point in the __dividend__.

Summary

When do you need to annex zeros when computing with decimals? See students' work.

_____
_____
_____
_____
_____
_____

Lesson 3 Divide Whole Numbers by Fractions
English Learner Instructional Strategy

Vocabulary Support: Frontload Academic Vocabulary

Write the word *reciprocal* and the Spanish cognate, *recíproco,* on the board. Then write $\frac{2}{3} \times \frac{3}{2} = ?$ Ask students to solve. *What is the answer?* **1** Repeat with another example. Explain that *reciprocals* are any two numbers with a product of one. Check students' understanding by giving examples and non-examples of reciprocals. Write *reciprocals* and a math example on the Word Wall.

Give each student the 2 through 10 cards from a set of number cards. Have one student use two cards to create a fraction. A partner must use his or her cards to create the reciprocal of that fraction. Switch roles and repeat several times.

English Language Development Leveled Activities

Entering/Emerging	Developing/Expanding	Bridging
Recognize and Act It Out	**Memorize the Rule**	**Academic Language**
Write $3 \div \frac{1}{3}$. Use three equal-sized strips of construction paper to represent 3. Have the class count the sections. Say, *There are three whole sections in the number 3. We will find how many $\frac{1}{3}$ sections there are in 3.* Fold each strip of construction paper into three equal-sized sections. Explain that each section represents $\frac{1}{3}$. Have the students count the sections. Say, *There are 9 one-third sections in 3.* Write $= 9$ beside the original expression. Give students construction paper to model the expression $5 \div \frac{1}{2}$ independently.	Write *divide, whole number, fraction, multiply, reciprocal.* Review the terms, and have a student draw a picture or a math example to illustrate each. Review how to divide a whole number by a fraction by completing some examples. Then write these five phrases on separate index cards: *to divide a; whole number by; a fraction; multiply by; its reciprocal.* Have students shuffle the cards and arrange them in the correct order to describe how to divide a whole number by a fraction. For this activity, students must use both math and language skills. Provide an extra challenge by having students write the rule from memory.	Create two piles of cards. One pile has a whole number written on each card. The second pile has a fraction written on each card. Have pairs choose one card from each pile. Say, *Divide the whole number by the fraction.* Encourage pairs to model with bar diagrams or fraction tiles. One student in each pair will work to find the quotient. The other student will list the steps taken and will check the answer using multiplication. Have pairs switch roles and repeat the activity using new cards.

Teacher Notes:

NAME _____ DATE _____ PERIOD _____

Lesson 3 Vocabulary

Divide Whole Numbers by Fractions

Use the definition map to list qualities about the vocabulary word or phrase. Sample answers are given.

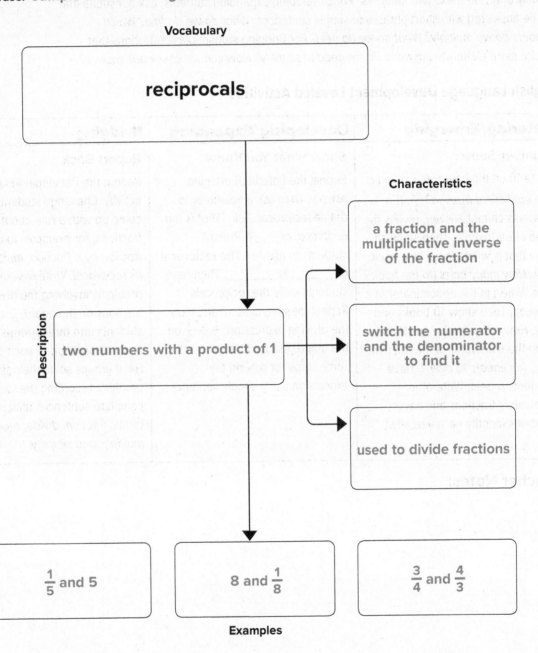

Vocabulary

reciprocals

Description

two numbers with a product of 1

Characteristics

a fraction and the multiplicative inverse of the fraction

switch the numerator and the denominator to find it

used to divide fractions

Examples

$\frac{1}{5}$ and 5

8 and $\frac{1}{8}$

$\frac{3}{4}$ and $\frac{4}{3}$

Course 1 · Module 3 *Compute with Multi-Digit Numbers and Fractions* **17**

Lesson 4 Divide Fractions by Fractions
English Learner Instructional Strategies

Language Structure Support: Tiered Questions

Gear questions to elicit responses that align with students' levels of English proficiency. Entering/Emerging students may be able to respond only with gestures or single-word answers, so ask questions such as: *Do we divide by 3 or 4? Show me the numerators. Do we multiply or divide these two numbers?* For Developing/Expanding students, ask questions that can be answered with short phrases or simple sentences: *What do we do first? Which numbers do we multiply? What do we do next?* For Bridging students, ask questions that require more elaborate answers: *Do we need to simplify? How can we check our answer?*

English Language Development Leveled Activities

Entering/Emerging	Developing/Expanding	Bridging
Number Sense	**Show What You Know**	**Report Back**
Write 10 on the board. Ask, *What is the equivalent fraction?* $\frac{10}{1}$. If students cannot answer, review the idea of part/whole. Then show an item that is whole, such as a book. Ask, *How many parts (to the book)?* **one** Write 1 in the denominator of a fraction. Then show 10 books and ask, *How many books?* **ten** Write 10 in the numerator of the fraction. Say, *Ten equals 10 over 1.* Have students repeat. Write other equivalent fractions and have students identify each verbally.	Repeat the Entering/Emerging activity. Then ask a volunteer to define *reciprocal*. Ask, *What is the reciprocal of ____?* Prompt students to answer, **The reciprocal of _____ is _____.** Then have students write the reciprocals. Repeat for several numbers. Write the division expression: $\frac{3}{4} \div \frac{1}{8}$ on the board. Ask partners to create some steps for solving the expression using simple sentences.	Repeat the Developing/Expanding activity. Challenge students to come up with a rule about dividing fractions; for example, *To divide a fraction by a fraction, multiply by its reciprocal.* Write several problems involving the division of fractions on the board. Organize students into three groups and assign a problem to each group. Have groups solve their assigned problem, recording the steps in complete sentences utilizing these terms: *fraction, divide, reciprocal, multiply, and simplify.*

Teacher Notes:

NAME _____ DATE _____ PERIOD _____

Lesson 4 Vocabulary
Divide Fractions by Fractions

Use the word cards to define each vocabulary word and give an example. **Sample answers are given.**

Word Card

quotient	el cociente
Definition	**Definición**
The result of a division problem.	Resultado de un problema de división.

Example Sentence
Holly is making $\frac{1}{2}$ of a batch of cookies. The recipe calls for $\frac{2}{3}$ cups of sugar. She divided $\frac{2}{3}$ by $\frac{1}{2}$ and found that she needed $\frac{3}{8}$ cup of sugar.

Word Card

reciprocal	recíproco
Definition	**Definición**
Any two numbers that have a product of 1.	Cualquier par de números cuyo producto es 1.

Example Sentence
When you divide by a fraction (such as $\frac{2}{3}$), it is the same as multiplying by the reciprocal of the fraction $\left(\frac{3}{2}\right)$.

Lesson 5 Divide with Whole and Mixed Numbers

English Learner Instructional Strategies

Graphic Support: Tables

Have students create a four-column chart in their math notebooks, labeling the columns as follows: *Dividend, Divisor, Division Sentence,* and *Quotient in Simplest Form.* Review any of the vocabulary, as necessary. As students complete division problems, have them plug in the information for columns 1–3. After performing the operation, they should fill in column 4. Remind students to include unit measurements in their answers, where they apply. Assign a bridging student to work with emerging and expanding pairs as a facilitator to guide the other students as needed using simple questions, such as, **What is the number we divide by? What is the number we need to divide? How do we divide by a mixed/whole number?**

English Language Development Leveled Activities

Entering/Emerging	Developing/Expanding	Bridging
Word Knowledge Write $3\frac{1}{4}$. Say, *Point to the whole number. Point to the fraction. A number with a whole number and fraction is a mixed number.* Prompt students to say, **mixed number.** Write $\frac{13}{4}$. Ask, *What type of number is this?* Remind students that if the numerator is larger than the denominator, then it is an improper fraction. Model and prompt students to say, **improper fraction.** Model how students can use fraction tiles to discover equivalent mixed numbers and improper fractions.	**Show What You Know** Have students create a game sheet with two columns. In the first column, they should write several division expressions that include division by both whole and mixed numbers. In the second column, they should write the corresponding multiplication expressions in a different order. Students exchange game sheets and complete the sheets by drawing a line from the division expression to the matching multiplication expression. Students can then check each other's work using the following language: **Great job! You got them all correct!** or **I don't think this is correct. Please check this again. The answer is not ____.**	**Make Connections** Have students look in newspapers for mixed numbers. Then have them discuss a scenario in which that number would be the divisor. Ask, *Why would you want to divide by that number?* Students might use the context of the article in the newspaper where they found the number or come up with their own story. Have students write their own real-world problem involving the numbers they find. Then have them trade with another student who should perform the operation. You might compile and distribute the problems to everyone in the class.

Teacher Notes:

NAME _____ DATE _____ PERIOD _____

Lesson 5 Review Vocabulary

Divide with Whole and Mixed Numbers

Use the vocabulary squares to write a definition, a sentence, and an example for each vocabulary word.

	Definition
divisor	a number that another number is divided by
Example Circle the divisor. $500 \div 2\frac{1}{2} = 200$	**Sentence** In the equation $500 \div 2\frac{1}{2} = 200$, $2\frac{1}{2}$ is the divisor.

	Definition
dividend	the number that is being divided
Example Circle the dividend. $500 \div 2\frac{1}{2} = 200$	**Sentence** In the equation $500 \div 2\frac{1}{2} = 200$, 500 is the dividend.

	Definition
quotient	the answer to a division problem
Example Circle the quotient. $500 \div 2\frac{1}{2} = 200$	**Sentence** In the equation $500 \div 2\frac{1}{2} = 200$, 200 is the quotient.

Course 1 • Module 3 *Compute with Multi-Digit Numbers and Fractions* **19**

Lesson 1 Represent Integers
English Learner Instructional Strategy

Sensory Support: Total Physical Response

Use tape to create a giant number line on the floor. Create a set of integer index cards, from −10 to 10. Show each card to students and have them name it, including the words *positive* and *negative*. After you have finished drilling all of the numbers say, *These are integers.* Write *integer, positive integer,* and *negative integer* on the Word Wall with examples.

Distribute a card to each student, and have them take turns naming the integer and placing it on the giant number line. Ask a student, *How far is 3 from zero?* Students can count back on the number line to discover that the number 3 is three away from zero. Ask, *How far is −3 from zero?* Have students count up to zero to arrive at the same result. Say, *3 and −3 are opposites.* Repeat for other opposite numbers. Write *opposites* on the Word Wall with an example.

English Language Development Leveled Activities

Entering/Emerging	Developing/Expanding	Bridging
Number Sense	**Number Sense**	**Signal Words**
Give each pair of students a set of shuffled integer cards from −10 to 10. As they turn over each card, have them say the name of the integer on the card, including *positive* or *negative*. Then have them work together to order the cards from least to greatest. Encourage comparison language, such as _____ **is [greater/less] than _____.**	Give each pair of students a set of integer cards from −10 to 10, including zero. Have partners take turns drawing an integer card. The student must first say the integer name, including *positive* or *negative*. Then the student should write the number on a number line. Have students ask and answer the following question: **Which number is the opposite of _____?**	Ask, *How would you define a negative number?* **A negative number is a number less than 0.** *How do you write a negative number?* **Use the negative sign before the number.** Have a volunteer write several negative numbers on the board. Then create a list of words they might encounter that signal increases or decreases. For example, **Increase:** *add, above, over, gain;* **Decrease:** *below, subtract, under, loss.* Post the list of words on the Word Wall. Encourage students to add words to the list as they encounter them.

Multicultural Teacher Tip

In Mexico and Latin American countries, negative numbers can be represented two different ways: with a negative sign in front of the number (i.e. −3) or with a horizontal line directly above the number (i.e. $\overline{3}$). The latter approach may be confusing, as it is also the common format for representing repeating decimals.

NAME _____ DATE _____ PERIOD _____

Lesson 1 Vocabulary

Represent Integers

Use the vocabulary squares to write a definition, a sentence, and an example
for each vocabulary word. Sample answers are given.

	Definition
integer	any number from the set {... −4, −3, −2, −1, 0, 1, 2, 3, 4 ...} where ... means continues without end
Example	**Sentence**
5, 31, 0, −3, −64	Whole numbers and their opposites are all integers.

	Definition
positive integer	a whole number that is greater than zero; can be written with or without a "+" sign
Example	**Sentence**
7, 13, 654	I can count the number of people in the room using positive integers.

	Definition
negative integer	the opposite of a natural number; It is less than zero. It is written with a "−" sign.
Example	**Sentence**
−6, −75, −1,647	The numbers −2, −4, −17, and −34 are negative integers.

Lesson 2 Opposites and Absolute Value
English Learner Instructional Strategy

Sensory Support: Mnemonics

Write *absolute value* and *graph* and their Spanish cognates, *valor absoluto* and *graficar*, respectively. Introduce the words, and provide math examples to support understanding. Utilize other appropriate translation tools for non-Spanish speaking ELLs. Discuss how *absolute, value,* and *graph* are all multiple-meaning words in English. Ensure students understand that, within a math context, *absolute* means "unchanging," *value* means "quantity," and *graph* means "to plot a point."

On the board, write |4| and |−4|. Then draw a number line and model how to find the absolute values of |4| and |−4|. Point out the lines on both sides of an integer, which show that the integer's value is absolute. Write and then say: *When I believe something **absolutely**, I am **positive**, or sure, that I am correct.* Tell students they can use this sentence as a device for remembering that the value of an absolute number is always positive.

English Language Development Leveled Activities

Entering/Emerging	Developing/Expanding	Bridging
Look, Listen, and Respond	**Listen and Write**	**Share What You Know**
Give each pair of students a set of shuffled integer cards from −10 to 10, including zero. As they turn over each card, have them say the name of the integer on the card, including *positive* or *negative*. Then have them write the number on a number line. Finally, remind students that the distance from zero is the absolute value. As you say two integers, have students give thumbs up for *same absolute value* or thumbs down for *not the same absolute value*. Say, *Thumbs up if the absolute value is the **same**. Thumbs down if not.*	As you dictate a list of integers, have students write them in their math notebooks. Then have students independently write the opposite integer for each one. Have students draw a number line and plot each integer and its opposite on the line and compare number lines with a partner. Finally, remind students that the distance from zero is the absolute value. Ask students for the absolute value of various numbers. They may consult their number lines as needed. Have them use the sentence frame: **The absolute value of _____ is _____.**	Have Bridging students partner with Entering/Emerging or Developing/Expanding students. The bridging partner should be able to help his or her partner understand unknown vocabulary. If necessary, they can ask you clarifying questions, such as, **What does _____ mean? Does _____ mean _____?** Students can draw a horizontal or vertical number line in order to visualize direction. Have them label items in their drawings as well as the numbers associated with the stories.

Teacher Notes:

NAME _____ DATE _____ PERIOD _____

Lesson 2 Vocabulary
Opposites and Absolute Value

Use the word cards to define each vocabulary word or phrase and give an example. Sample answers are given.

Word Cards

absolute value	valor absoluto
Definition	**Definición**
the distance between a number and zero on a number line	distancia entre un número y cero en la recta numérica.
Example Sentence	
Sample answer: The absolute value of 2 is 2. The absolute value of −2 is 2.	

Copyright © McGraw-Hill Education

Word Cards

opposites	opuestos
Definition	**Definición**
Integers are opposites if they are the same distance from zero in opposite directions.	Los enteros son opuestos si son la misma distancia de cero en direcciones opuestas.
Example Sentence	
Sample answer: The numbers −2 and 2 are opposites.	
−2 + 2 = 0	

Copyright © McGraw-Hill Education

Course 1 · Module 4 *Integers, Rational Numbers, and the Coordinate Plane* **21**

Copyright © McGraw-Hill Education.

Course 1 · Module 4 *Integers, Rational Numbers, and the Coordinate Plane* **21**

Lesson 3 Compare and Order Integers
English Learner Instructional Strategy

Language Structure Support: Language for Comparing

Ask two students to stand next to each other. Ask the group, *Is [student 1 name] taller, or is [student 2 name] taller?* After students answer, say, *[Student name] is taller than [student name].* Have students repeat the sentence. Repeat with other examples.

Tell students that when comparing two things, we use comparative adjectives to describe them. Elicit different adjectives and their opposites: *big/small, long/short, tall/short, low/high, old/young.* Teach them how to add the comparative ending *-er* to each word.

Finally, check students' concept of which words will likely have a larger value on a number line. For example, if we say someone is younger, then he would fall lower on a number line than someone who is older. Review several examples.

English Language Development Leveled Activities

Entering/Emerging	Developing/Expanding	Bridging
Number Sense Give each pair of students a set of integer cards from −10 to 10, including zero. Have students shuffle the cards. As they turn over each card, have them say the name of the integer on the card, including *positive* or *negative*. Then have them work together to order the cards from lowest to highest. Encourage comparison language, such as, **No, this is greater. _____ is [greater/less] than _____.**	**Look and Say** Give each pair of students a set of integer cards from −10 to 10, including zero. Have students create their own cards for > and < signs. Review the >, < symbols. Write 2 and −5 on the board with a space in between. Ask, *Which number is greater?* **2** Model how to draw the correct sign, 2 > −5. Tell students that the sign always wants to "eat" the greater number. Prompt students to say, **Two is greater than negative five.** Have partners turn two integer cards face up on the desk, determine which sign (> or <) should go between them, and then say the inequality: _____ **is [greater/less] than** _____. Repeat until firm.	**Building Oral Language** Write a set of numbers on the board; for example, {−8, 4, −2, 0}. Point to the braces and say, *These are braces. They are used to show a set of numbers.* Have students repeat. Have partners draw a number line and plot the numbers. Then have them describe the numbers using language for comparing and contrasting: _____ **is greater than** _____, **but it is less than** _____. _____ **is a [positive/negative] number, so it is [greater/less] than** _____. **Even though** _____ **is a [positive/negative number], it is [greater/less] than** _____.

Teacher Notes:

Lesson 3 Notetaking
Compare and Order Integers

Use Cornell notes to better understand the lesson's concepts. Complete each
sentence by filling in the blanks with the correct word or phrase.

Questions	Notes
1. How do I compare integers?	I can compare signs. __Positive__ numbers are greater than __negative__ numbers. I can compare position on the number line. Greater numbers are graphed farther to the __right__.
2. How do I order integers?	I can use a __number line__ to order a set of integers. I can compare __signs__ and __absolute values__ to order a set of integers.

Summary

How can symbols and absolute value help you to order sets of integers? **See students' work.**

_____

_____

_____

_____

_____

_____

_____

Lesson 4 Rational Numbers

English Learner Instructional Strategy

Collaborative Support: Think-Pair-Share

Have students work in pairs as they practice comparing and ordering rational numbers. Have one student compare the numbers by converting all fractions to decimals. The other student should use manipulatives or a number line to compare and order the rational numbers. In some cases, they may be able to easily convert a decimal to a fraction and then use fraction tiles to compare. Once both students have arrived at a conclusion, have them compare answers and then share with the group. Encourage the following language as students give their explanations:

Entering/Emerging: _____ is [greater/less] than _____.

Developing/Expanding: **I compared** _____ **and** _____. **I changed the fraction** _____ **to a decimal.** _____ **is [greater/less] than** _____.

Bridging: **I know that** $\frac{3}{4}$ **equals 0.75, so** $\frac{3}{4}$ **is greater than 0.5.**

English Language Development Leveled Activities

Entering/Emerging	Developing/Expanding	Bridging
Look and Compare Write $\frac{2}{3}$ and $\frac{3}{5}$ on the board. Ask, *Which is greater?* Then model using fraction tiles to compare. Couple two $\frac{1}{3}$ tiles and three $\frac{1}{5}$ tiles. Compare lengths. Ask, *Which is longer?* Students should be able to identify that $\frac{2}{3}$ is longer than $\frac{3}{5}$. Model and prompt, $\frac{2}{3}$ **is greater than** $\frac{3}{5}$. Have partners work with fraction tiles to compare different rational numbers that you write on the board. Have them order them from smallest to largest.	**Developing Oral Language** Provide pairs of students with a set of ten index cards, each with a rational number on it. Have partners put the cards in order from least to greatest. Have fraction tiles, number lines, and paper and pencil available. Have students explain how they ordered the numbers using sentence frames such as, **We converted all** _____ **to** _____. **We compared fraction tiles for** _____ **and** _____. **[Smaller/Greater] numbers are on the** _____ **on a number line.** Have pairs exchange cards and repeat the activity.	**Building Oral Language** Have students work in groups of three. Have student A choose any numerator and student B the denominator. Student C will find the decimal equivalent of the fraction. Have groups repeat the process, switching roles each time. Then have them compare and order the rational numbers they created. Have one student in each group describe the numbers using language such as, **I know** _____ **is equivalent to** _____ **because** _____. **We know that** _____ **is [greater/less] than** _____ **because the decimal value is [greater/lesser].**

Teacher Notes:

NAME _____ DATE _____ PERIOD _____

Lesson 4 Notetaking
Rational Numbers

Use Cornell notes to better understand the lesson's concepts. Complete each
sentence by filling in the blanks with the correct word or phrase.

Questions	Notes
1. What is a rational number?	A rational number is any number that can be written as a _____**fraction**_____ $\frac{a}{b}$, where a and b are _____**integers**_____, and b _____$\neq 0$_____.
2. How do I compare and order rational numbers?	First I can write the rational numbers in the same _____**form**_____. Then I can use a _____**number line**_____ to compare and order the numbers.

Summary
How can a number line help in ordering rational numbers? **See students' work.**

Course 1 · **Module 4** *Integers, Rational Numbers, and the Coordinate Plane*   **23**

Lesson 5 The Coordinate Plane
English Learner Instructional Strategy

Graphic Support: Coordinate Planes

Draw a coordinate plane on the board. Review the following terms (and cognates, if applicable) on the Word Wall: *coordinate plane (plano de coordenadas), origin (origen), x-axis, y-axis, ordered pair (par ordenado), x-coordinate (coordenada x), y-coordinate (coordenada y),* and *graph (gráfica).* Outline each quadrant in a different color. Point to a quadrant and say, *This is a quadrant.* Prompt students to repeat, **quadrant.** Underline *quad* and say, *Quad means "four."* How many quadrants in the coordinate plane? **four** Identify Quadrants I, II, III, and IV. Add *quadrant* and its Spanish cognate, *cuadrante,* to the Word Wall with a pictorial example.

Make laminated copies of a coordinate plane, enough for each student. Have students use a board marker and the coordinate plane as they work on related exercises.

English Language Development Leveled Activities

Entering/Emerging	Developing/Expanding	Bridging
Developing Oral Language	**Developing Oral Language**	**Building Oral Language**
On a laminated coordinate plane, one partner should secretly plot three points, then identify each point by writing the corresponding ordered pair at the bottom of the coordinate plane. Then have the student give their partner the location of the first point by saying, **The x-coordinate is ____. The y-coordinate is ____.** Have the partner plot the point on his or her own grid. Continue for the remaining two points. Have partners compare coordinate planes. Switch roles and repeat.	Ask each student to draw a simple shape with straight sides on a coordinate plane. They should place the corners of the shape on definable points on the plane. Have one student dictate an ordered pair to a partner, using the sentence frame, **The [first/second/third] point is located at ____.** Then challenge them to use the ordered pairs to reproduce each other's shapes on new coordinate planes.	On a laminated coordinate plane, ask each student to secretly draw a triangle on the plane. They should place the vertices on definable points on the plane. Partners should take turns asking and answering questions to guess the location of each vertex of their partner's triangle. **Which quadrant is the first point in? Is the x-coordinate [greater/less] than ____? Is the x-coordinate ____?** Check that students speak in complete sentences.

Multicultural Teacher Tip

You may experience ELLs who appear to listen closely to your instructions and indicate that they understand but it becomes clear later in the lesson that they did not. This may be due to a student coming from a culture in which the teacher is regarded as a strong authority figure. They may be reluctant to ask questions, considering it impolite and an implication that the teacher is failing.

NAME _____ DATE _____ PERIOD _____

Lesson 5 Vocabulary
The Coordinate Plane

Use the concept web to identify the quadrants of the coordinate plane. Write an ordered pair to name a point in each quadrant. Sample points are given.

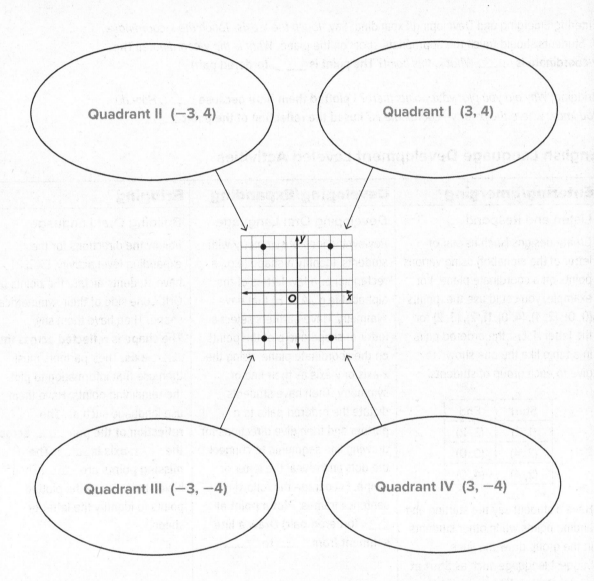

Lesson 6 Graph Reflections of Points

English Learner Instructional Strategy

Language Structure Support: Tiered Language

Review all terms associated with the coordinate plane on the Word Wall. Introduce the term *reflection*. Show students a mirror. Point out your reflection in it. Then draw half of a smiley face on the board. Use the mirror to create the other side of the face. Say, *The reflection shows the same parts of the face on the other side.* Add *reflection* to the Word Wall with a pictorial example. As you work through the lesson, use level-appropriate language:

Entering/Emerging and Developing/Expanding: Say, *Touch the x-axis. Touch the x-coordinate, 4.* Students should touch the appropriate spots on the plane. *What is the y-coordinate?* **The y-coordinate is _____.** *What is this point?* **The point is _____. (ordered pair)**

Bridging: *Why did you plot your points there?* **I plotted them here because _____.** *How do you know where the [x- or y-] coordinate is?* **I used the reflection of the point _____.**

English Language Development Leveled Activities

Entering/Emerging	Developing/Expanding	Bridging
Listen and Respond Create designs (such as star or letter of the alphabet) using various points on a coordinate plane. For example, you could use the points (0, 0), (2, 4), (4, 0), (1, 2), (3, 2) for the letter *A*. List the ordered pairs in a table like the one shown to give to each group of students.	**Developing Oral Language** Review the idea of *symmetry* with students. Identify a shape (e.g., a rectangle) or a few letters of the alphabet (e.g., A or H) that have symmetry. Have partners select a letter or shape and plot the points on the coordinate plane, using the x-axis or y-axis as their line of symmetry. Then have students dictate the ordered pairs to a partner and then give directions for drawing line segments to connect the dots and reveal the letter or shape. Encourage the following sentence frames: **Plot a point at _____. (ordered pair) Draw a line segment from _____ to _____.**	**Building Oral Language** Follow the directions for the expanding level activity, EXCEPT have students dictate the points on ONLY one side of their symmetrical shape. Then have them say, **The shape is reflected across the _____-axis.** Their partners must then use that information to plot the remaining points. Have them use language such as, **The reflection of the pair _____ across the _____-axis is _____. The missing points are _____.** Then have students use the plotted points to identify the letter or shape.

Table in Entering/Emerging column:

Start	End
(1, 2)	(3, 2)
(2, 4)	(0, 0)
(2, 4)	(4, 0)

Have a student say the starting and ending points while other students in the group draw the lines. Suggest language such as **Start at _____. Draw a line segment to _____. Switch roles and repeat with other shapes.**

Teacher Notes:

NAME _____ DATE _____ PERIOD _____

Lesson 6 Review Vocabulary

Graph Reflections of Points

Complete the four-square chart to review the word or phrase. Then answer the question below. Sample answers are given.

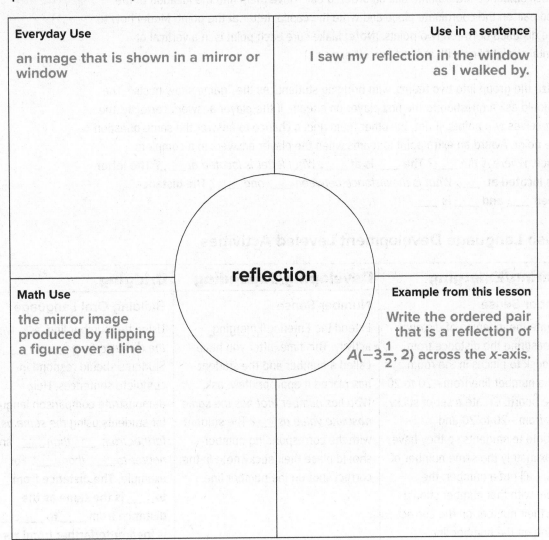

Everyday Use

an image that is shown in a mirror or window

Use in a sentence

I saw my reflection in the window as I walked by.

reflection

Math Use

the mirror image produced by flipping a figure over a line

Example from this lesson

Write the ordered pair that is a reflection of $A\left(-3\frac{1}{2}, 2\right)$ across the x-axis.

What does it mean to reflect a point across the x-axis?

To find the mirror image of the point on the other side of the x-axis. The points

have the same x-coordinates and the y-coordinates are opposites.

_____

_____

Course 1 · Module 4 *Integers, Rational Numbers, and the Coordinate Plane* **25**

Lesson 7 Absolute Value and Distance
English Learner Instructional Strategies

Collaborative Support: Hands-On Game

Create a large, four-quadrant coordinate plane on the board. Review the terms *coordinate plane, quadrant.* Label Quadrants I, II, III, and IV. Have students point to the correct quadrant.

Give each student a letter name and an ordered pair. Have them find the location of the ordered pair on the coordinate plane and write the capital letter at the point. Model how to find the distance between two points. (**Note:** Make sure each point is in a vertical or horizontal straight line with at least one other point.)

Organize the group into two teams, with bridging students as the "game show hosts." The host should ask a question to the first player on a team. If the player answers correctly, the team receives two points. If not, the other team gets a chance to answer the same question for one point. Award an extra point to teams when the player answers in a complete sentence. *Where is the ____?* **The ____ is at ____.** *What letter is located at ____?* **The letter ____ is located at ____.** *What is the distance between ____ and ____?* **The distance between ____ and ____ is ____.**

English Language Development Leveled Activities

Entering/Emerging	Developing/Expanding	Bridging
Number Sense	**Number Sense**	**Building Oral Language**
Illustrate the meaning of *distance* by measuring the distance from your desk to places in the room. Draw a number line from −20 to 20 on the board. Create a set of sticky notes from −20 to 20 and distribute to students so they have approximately the same number of notes. Call out a number; the student with that number should place their number on the correct position on the number line. Demonstrate how to find the distance from that number to zero by counting on the number line. Ask, *What is the distance from zero?* Students may respond with just one word or the frame, **The distance is ____.** Review the idea that absolute value is a number's distance from zero.	Extend the Entering/Emerging activity. This time, after you have called a number and the student has placed it appropriately, ask, *Who has number that has the same absolute value as ___?* The student with the corresponding number should place their sticky note in the correct spot on the number line.	Using the number line, ask, *What is the distance from ____ to ____?* Students should respond in complete sentences. Help demonstrate comparison language for students using *the same as, farther from ____ than ____,* and *nearer to ____ than ____.* For example, **The distance from ____ to ____ is the same as the distance from ____ to ____. ____ is [nearer to/farther from] zero than ____.**

NAME _____ DATE _____ PERIOD _____

Lesson 7 Vocabulary
Absolute Value and Distance

Use the three-column chart to organize the vocabulary in this lesson. Write the word in Spanish. Then write the correct terms to complete each definition using a word from the word bank.

Word Bank						
distance	four	ordered pair	origin	points	space	zero (0)

English	Spanish	Definition
absolute value	valor absoluto	The ___distance___ of a number from ___zero (0)___ on a number line.
coordinate plane	plano coordinada	The plane created by the perpendicular intersection of a horizontal number line and a vertical number line. The ___origin___ is where the number lines intersect. Each point on a coordinate plane can be labeled with a(n) ___ordered pair___.
distance	distancia	The amount of ___space___ between two ___points___.
quadrant	cuadrante	One of the ___four___ sectors in a coordinate plane.

26 **Course 1 · Module 4** *Integers, Rational Numbers, and the Coordinate Plane*

Lesson 1 Powers and Exponents

English Learner Instructional Strategy

Language Structure Support: Tiered Questions

Write *base* and *exponent* and the Spanish cognates, *base* and *exponente,* on the Word Wall. Write 2^3 and have students identify the base and the exponent.

During the lesson, be sure to ask questions according to ELLs' level of English proficiency. For example, ask Entering/Emerging students simple questions that elicit one-word answers or allow the student to respond with a gesture: *Which number is the power? Is this the base? Do I use _____ as a factor _____ times or _____times?* For Developin/Expanding students, ask questions that elicit answers in the form of simple phrases or short sentences: *How do I know which number to multiply? What do I need to do first? or Which numbers are the exponents?* For Bridging students, ask questions that require more complex answers: *Why is _____ used as a factor _____ times?*

English Language Development Leveled Activities

Entering/Emerging	Developing/Expanding	Bridging
Academic Vocabulary	**Act It Out**	**Deductive Reasoning**
Guide students to create a classroom anchor chart with visual examples and labels for *power, base,* and *exponent.* As you provide an example for each word and identify it, have students chorally repeat the vocabulary word. Monitor correct pronunciation and repeat the modeling as needed. Listen to how students are saying *power,* as the /ow/ sound is not used in Spanish and may be troublesome.	Divide students into groups of 3-4. Distribute a pair of number cubes to each group. Say, *Roll your number cubes to create a power. Use the greater number as the base and the lesser number as the exponent. Write the power and find its value.* Give students time to complete the task. Then have students take turns describing the power using the following sentence frames: **The base is _____. The exponent is _____. The power is _____. The value of the power is _____.**	Write the following on the board: 2^2, 3^2, 4^2, 5^2, 6^2, 7^2, 8^2, 9^2, 10^2. Ask students to name the base and the exponent for each. Then assign one of the numbers to each pair of students. Have them use manipulatives to discover why a number to the 2nd power is called a *perfect square.*

Multicultural Teacher Tip

Mathematical notation varies from culture to culture, so you may find ELLs using unfamiliar symbols. For example, students from Latin American countries may use a point in place of $\times$ to indicate multiplication. Although the point is also commonly used in the U.S., the placement and size may vary depending on the student's native culture. In Mexico, the point is larger and set higher between the numbers than in the U.S. In other countries, the point is set low and can be confused with a decimal point.

NAME _____ DATE _____ PERIOD _____

Lesson 1 Vocabulary
Powers and Exponents

Use the three-column chart to organize the vocabulary in this lesson. Write the word in Spanish. Then write the definition of each word. Sample answers are given.

English	Spanish	Definition
base	base	the number used as a factor
exponent	exponente	the number that tells how many times the base is used as a factor
factors	factores	the numbers being multiplied in a product
powers	potencias	numbers expressed using exponents

Lesson 2 Numerical Expressions

English Learner Instructional Strategy

Collaborative Support: Round the Table

Organize students into small groups. Write the following problem on the board:
$55 \div 11 + 7 \cdot (2^2 + 14) =$ _____. Have one student in each group write the problem on a large
piece of paper. Then have students work jointly to simplify the expression by passing the paper
around the table. Each student will perform one step in simplifying the expression using the
order of operations. Remind students to 1) simplify inside parentheses first, 2) find the value of
all powers, 3) multiply or divide from left to right, and 4) add and subtract from left to right. As
they work, each student will write a sentence describing his or her step. Provide the following
sentence frames:

**First, we _____ inside parentheses. Then we [multiplied/divided] _____. Then we [added/
subtracted] _____.**

English Language Development Leveled Activities

Entering/Emerging	Developing/Expanding	Bridging
Mnemonic Device	**Mnemonic Device**	**Logical Reasoning**
Write *order of operations* and its Spanish cognate, *orden de las operaciones*, on the board. After practicing the order of operations in a few examples from the lesson, teach students the mnemonic device PEMDAS to help them remember the correct order: **P**arentheses (or grouping), **E**xponents, **M**ultiply, **D**ivide, **A**dd, **S**ubtract. A common saying to remember these letters is **P**lease **E**xcuse **M**y **D**ear **A**unt **S**ally. Have fun trying to come up with a new, more meaningful mnemonic device with students!	Give each student an index card with one of the following words on it: **P**arentheses, **E**xponents, **M**ultiply, **D**ivide, **A**dd, **S**ubtract. Then write this numerical expression: $35 \div 5 + 4^2 \cdot (10 - 7) - 3$. Say, *What do we do first? Hold up your card.* A student holding a Parentheses card should come to the front and simplify the expression inside the parentheses. As they do, encourage them to describe the step: **First I _____.** Then say, *What is next?* The student holding an Exponents card should do the next step in the same manner. Continue for all steps. Repeat with another expression.	Write the following question on the board: *Why is order of operations important?* Have students work in groups of three to brainstorm possible answers. One student should take notes. Then have students use the notes to write an answer that is at least two sentences long. If students need suggestions, ask follow-up questions, such as *What would happen if we add before we multiply?* Have students present their answers to the group. Discuss any differences or similarities in the groups' answers.

Teacher Notes:

NAME _____ DATE _____ PERIOD _____

Lesson 2 Vocabulary
Numerical Expressions

Use the word cards to define each vocabulary word or phrase and give an example. Sample answers are given.

Word Cards

numerical expression	expressión numérica
Definition	**Definición**
a combination of numbers and operations	una combinación de númerous y operaciones
Example Sentence	
You can use a numerical expression, to describe the cost of three $10 pizza delivered with a $5 delivery charge.	

Word Cards

order of operations	orden de las operaciones
Definition	**Definición**
rules that tell which operation to perform first	reglas que establecen cuál operación debes realizer primero
Example Sentence	
The order of operations tells you to simplify multiplication first, then addition in the expression $5 + 3 \times 10$.	

Lesson 3 Write Algebraic Expressions
English Learner Instructional Strategy

Graphic Support: Bar Diagrams

Write the following expressions on the board: *eight dollars more than Ryan earned, 10 dollars less than the original price,* and *four times the number of gallons.* Have students write the expressions on a piece of paper and then circle the signal words in each one (more than, less than, times). For each expression, ask, *What operations will you use?* Then encourage students to draw a representation of the problem at hand in the form of a bar diagram. For each expression, have them draw the diagram and then compare it with a partners' diagram.

Then ask, *What is the value that you do **not** know?* After students answer, tell them that this unknown value will be the variable in the expression. Say, *You just **defined the variable**.* Have students repeat the phrase. Write *define the variable* and its Spanish cognate, *definir la variable,* on the board and on the Word Wall. Have students use their bar diagrams and their variable to write an expression. Then compare with a partner and discuss the reasons for any differences.

English Language Development Leveled Activities

Entering/Emerging	Developing/Expanding	Bridging
Word Recognition	**Turn & Talk**	**Public Speaking Norms**
Write each of the following words and phrases on its own index card: *5 more than, and, 3 less than, 11 fewer than, plus, 4 times as many, $\frac{1}{2}$ as many, 8 times as much, 13 times more than, minus, divided equally.* Review as necessary. Have partners sort the cards according to the operation that they signal.	Ask students, *What is a variable?* **A symbol that represents a number.** Ask, *Do we know what the value of a variable is?* **no** Read this example phrase: *4 more chickens than Farmer Andy.* As you read the phrase, have partners turn and talk about what the variable in the phrase is. Ask, *Do you know how many chickens Farmer Andy has?* **no** Then the number of Farmer Andy's chickens is your variable. Present other phrases such as, *3 times as much money as Sue, half as many puppies as Spot,* and *4 fewer diamonds than Donald.* Have partners compare answers as a group.	Repeat the expanding level activity. When they turn and talk with a partner, encourage them to use common language such as, **[I think/I'm pretty sure/I'm positive/I'm sure/I'm not sure, but I think] the answer is _____.** As they are comparing with the group, encourage the language, **I disagree because _____. I think you might be wrong about that. I'm in total agreement. I couldn't agree more.** Then have partners work together to write an expression (or for a further challenge, a scenario) for each phrase.

Teacher Notes:

NAME _____ DATE _____ PERIOD _____

Lesson 3 Notetaking
Write Algebraic Expressions

Use Cornell notes to better understand the lesson's concepts. Complete each sentence by filling in the blanks with the correct word or phrase.

Questions	Notes
1. How do I write phrases as algebraic expressions?	First, I ____describe____ the situation using only the most important words. Then, I choose a ____variable____ to represent the ____unknown____ quantity. Last, I translate the phrase into an ____algebraic expression____.
2. What is a two-step expression?	an algebraic ____expression____ containing two ____different____ operations

Summary

How can writing phrases as algebraic expressions help me solve problems?

See students' work.

_____

_____

_____

_____

_____

_____

Lesson 4 Evaluate Algebraic Expressions
English Learner Instructional Strategy

Vocabulary Support: Frontload Academic Vocabulary

Write 4x on the board. Point to the expression and ask, *What is the value?* Allow students to make some guesses. Point to x. Ask, *How many is x?* **We don't know.** *That's right. The x can represent any number.* Point to 4x again and write x = 3 next to it. *What is the value of 4x?* **12** Erase x = 3 and write x = 10. *What is the value of 4x?* **40** Point to x and say, *The x can change value. It is called a **variable**.* Tell students that *vary* means "to change." Have students say, **variable.** Point to 4x and say, *This is an **algebraic expression**. It has a variable and an operation.* Prompt students to say, **algebraic expression.** Check that students pronounce /j/ and not /g/ in *algebraic.* Say, *When we gave a **value** to x, we could **evaluate** the expression. We knew the value of 4x.* Prompt students to say, evaluate.

Add the following words and their Spanish cognates to the Word Wall with math examples for each: *algebraic expression (expresión algebraica), variable (variable), evaluate (evaluar).*

English Language Development Leveled Activities

Entering/Emerging	Developing/Expanding	Bridging
Word Knowledge	**Number Sense**	**Number Sense**
Review the words *variable* and *expression*. Remind students that a variable is a symbol (usually a letter) that is used to represent, or stand for, a number. Algebraic expressions are combinations of variables, numbers, and at least one operation. Then write the following expressions on the board: w + 3. Say to a volunteer, *Circle the expression. Underline the variable. What is the operation?* **addition** Repeat with the expressions, 11 − x, y × 2, 12 ÷ z.	Repeat the Entering/Emerging level activity. Review the meaning of *evaluate (evaluar).* Give each pair of students a number cube. One student should roll the number cube to determine the value of the variable. Have partners find the value of each expression. Then have them report to the group using the sentence frames: **The expression is ____. The value of the variable is ____. The value of the expression is ____.**	Repeat the Entering/Emerging level activity. Then have partners work together to invent a scenario for each algebraic expression. Model an example for w + 3: Amy has three more apples than Walter. If necessary, suggest the following sentence frames to assist students with their scenarios: *(w + 3)* ____ **has three more ____ than ____.** *(11 − x)* **We started with 11 ____ and ____ took some; I have the rest.** *(y × 2)* ____ **made twice as many ____ as ____.** *(12 ÷ z)* **We found 12 ____ and divided them equally among us.**

Teacher Notes:

NAME _____ DATE _____ PERIOD _____

Lesson 4 Vocabulary

Evaluate Algebraic Expressions

Use the three-column chart to organize the vocabulary in this lesson. Write the
word in Spanish. Then write the definition of each word. Sample answers are given.

English	Spanish	Definition
algebra	álgebra	a mathematical language of symbols, including variables
variable	variable	a symbol, usually a letter, used to represent a number
algebraic expression	expresión algebraica	a combination of variables, numbers, and at least one operation
evaluate	evaluar	to find the value of an algebraic expression by replacing variables with numbers

30 **Course 1 · Module 5** *Numerical and Algebraic Expressions*

Lesson 5 Factors and Multiples

English Learner Instructional Strategy

Collaborative Support: Partners Work/Pairs Check

As a way to encourage verbal communication during class, have ELL partners work together. Give each pair a multiplication table, up to 10 × 10. As you point to a number, say, *This is the product. What are the factors?* Have partners discuss the answer before you call on a student. Entering/Emerging students can point to the correct factors. Developing/Expanding students can say, _____ **and** _____. Prompt Bridging students to use this sentence frame: _____ **and** _____ **are factors of** _____. Then point to another number, and ask, *What are two multiples of* _____? Have partners discuss the answer first before you call on students to elicit tiered responses. Continue in this manner as you review factors and multiples.

Have the same partners work together during the lesson to complete assigned problems. One student should complete the first problem while the second acts as coach. Then have them switch roles for the next problem. After they have finished both problems, have them check their answers with another pair. When both pairs have agreed on the answers, ask them to shake hands and continue working in original pairs on the next problems.

English Language Development Leveled Activities

Entering/Emerging	Developing/Expanding	Bridging
Word Knowledge Demonstrate the word *common*. Gather two groups of manipulatives, such as paper clips and counters. Put an eraser in each group. Point and say, *Look at the groups. What is the same?* Students should notice that both groups have an eraser. Say, *Yes. The groups have the erasers* **in common**. Prompt students to say, **in common**. Demonstrate with other examples, such as comparing students' hair color, the subjects of two photographs, or two book covers. Prompt students by asking, *What do these have* **in common**? Then create two lists of numbers with one number appearing in both lists. Ask, *What number do the lists have in common?*	**Word Knowledge** Offer examples of *greatest* and *least* using different amounts of water or rice, or different numbers of manipulatives. For example, put different amounts of water in three cups of the same size. Ask, *Which cup has the most?* After students point to the correct cup, say, *Yes. That cup has the* **greatest** *amount of water.* Prompt students to say, **greatest**. Then ask students to point out the cup with the least amount of water. Say, *Yes. That cup has the* **least** *amount of water.* Prompt students to say, **least**. Point out the similarities between *greatest/biggest* and *least/ smallest*.	**Building Oral Language** Organize students into two groups. Have the students in one group work together to create a presentation that describes the steps for finding the least common multiple (LCM) of two numbers (such as 6 and 9). Each student in the group should have at least one speaking role in the presentation. Have the students in the other group create a presentation about finding the greatest common factor (GCF) of two numbers (such as 27 and 15). When each group gives its presentation, have the other students take notes and offer feedback about the vocabulary and language the group used.

Teacher Notes:

Lesson 5 Notetaking
Factors and Multiples

Use Cornell notes to better understand the lesson's concepts. Complete each sentence by filling in the blanks with the correct word or phrase.

Questions	Notes
1. How do you find the greatest common factor (GCF) of two numbers?	A ____**common factor**____ is a number that is a factor of two or more numbers. The greatest of the common factors of two or more numbers is the ____**greatest common factor (GCF)**____. The greatest common factor can be found by: 1. ____**listing the factors**____ 2. ____**making a factor tree**____ 3. ____**using prime factorization**____ Look for the ____**common**____ factors. Then identify the ____**greatest**____ common factor.
2. How do you find the least common multiple (LCM) of two numbers?	The least nonzero number that is a multiple of two of more numbers is the ____**least common multiple (LCM)**____ of the numbers. The least common multiple can be found by: 1. ____**listing the multiples**____ 2. ____**using a number line**____ Look for ____**common**____ multiples. Then identify the ____**least**____ common multiple.

Summary
When is it helpful to find the LCM to complete a math problem? **See students' work.** _____ _____ _____ _____

Lesson 6 Use The Distributive Property
English Learner Instructional Strategy

Vocabulary Support: Frontload Academic Vocabulary

Write *distribute* on the board. Model and prompt students to say the word. Ask, *Does anyone know what this means?* If no one can answer, say, *Distribute means "give out parts of something."* Demonstrate as you distribute some paper to students. You might also show a photo of a distribution center with trucks carrying goods in and out. Ask students for ideas of things that are distributed and have them model doing it.

Write the following expression on the board: $3(x + 1)$. Say, *Watch how I **distribute** the 3 through the expression x + 1.* Then model "distributing" as you expand the expression to $3x + 3$. Say, *This is called the Distributive Property of Multiplication.* Prompt students to say the term. Write it on the board, and underline *Distribut-* in *Distributive*. Say, *In this lesson we will use the Distributive Property of Multiplication. This rule involves separating an expression into **parts** before multiplying.* Repeat this explanation as you work through the examples in the lesson.

English Language Development Leveled Activities

Entering/Emerging	Developing/Expanding	Bridging
Sentence Frames	**Word Knowledge**	**Act It Out**
Write the following expression on the board: $5(x + 2)$. Point to the 5 and ask, *Do I distribute this?* Students should respond using the sentence frame **[Yes/No], you [should/should not] distribute the ____.** Repeat for *x* and 2. Repeat with other expressions.	Have students work in pairs to discuss the word *distribute*. Invite them to look up the word in a bilingual dictionary. Students should talk about what the word means and make a list of things that are distributed. Then have them look at a problem from the lesson and discuss what is being distributed and why the property is called the *Distributive Property of Multiplication*.	Encourage students to model or act out problems using the Distributive Property. For example, present students with the following situation: There are 12 bushes and six trees in a landscaper's design. She wants to create the same design for 10 lawns. How many total plants does she need? Have partners make an area model or use algebra tiles to illustrate the problem. If necessary, tell students that the landscaper needs to distribute $(12 + 6) \cdot 10 = 18 \cdot 10$ or 180 plants and then have them create the model.

Teacher Notes:

NAME _____ DATE _____ PERIOD _____

Lesson 6 Notetaking
Use the Distributive Property

Use Cornell notes to better understand the lesson's concepts. Complete each
answer by filling in the blanks with the correct word or phrase.

Questions	Notes
1. How do I use the Distributive Property?	I use the Distributive Property to _____multiply_____ a sum by a number. I _____multiply_____ each addend by the number outside the _____parentheses_____ .
2. How do I factor an expression?	I write each term of the expression using _____prime factorization_____ and identify the common factors. I rewrite each term using the _____greatest common factor (GCF)_____ . Then I use the _____Distributive Property_____ to write the expression as a product of the factors.

Summary
How can the Distributive Property help me to rewrite expressions? See students' work.

Lesson 7 Equivalent Algebraic Expressions
English Learner Instructional Strategy

Collaborative Support: Pass the Pen

Write the following story problem on the board: The farmer's market sells fruit baskets. Each basket has 3 apples and 1 pear. Use a to represent the cost of each apple. Use p to represent the cost of each pear. Write and simplify an expression that represents the total cost of 5 baskets.

Organize students into groups of three and have them work together. Give each student a pen of a different color. Have the group work together to determine the expression that is represented by the story. Have one student write the expression on a paper. The first student in the group will do the first step in evaluating the problem and then write a short sentence describing the step. The next student performs the next step and so on until the problem is solved. Encourage use of lesson vocabulary; *terms, like terms,* and *constant* in the following example frames:

I used the _____ Property. I combined _____. I [multiplied/added/simplified/etc.] _____ and _____.

English Language Development Leveled Activities

Entering/Emerging	Developing/Expanding	Bridging
Multiple-Meaning Words	**Word Recognition**	**Academic Word Knowledge**
Write the word *like* and ask, *What does this mean?* Allow students to brainstorm meanings. Point to the word and ask, *Do you like music?* Write a student's answer in a complete sentence: *Yes, I like music.* Erase *like* and change to *enjoy.* Model and prompt students to say the new sentence. Demonstrate another meaning of *like* by showing a photo of a puppy and another of a full-grown dog. Say, prompt, and write, *A puppy is like a small dog.* Erase *like* and write *the same as* in its place. Model and prompt the new sentence. During the lesson, remind students that *like terms* are terms with the **same** variable.	Have students create a set of vocabulary card pairs. On one card will be the vocabulary word and on the other should be an example of the word. For instance, for *coefficient,* the example card could have the following: $3v + 1$. The 3 can be written in red, circled, or otherwise highlighted. Have students create cards for the following vocabulary: *constant, variable, Distributive Property, Commutative Property, like terms, term, equivalent expressions.* Students can use the cards to play a matching game.	Assign one of the following vocabulary terms to a pair of students: *constant, variable, Distributive Property, Commutative Property, like terms, term, equivalent expressions.* Have the partners "write a report" in paragraph form about their term. Reports must include a definition, an example of the term, when the term is useful, and why it is used. Students can then plan a presentation and, as a pair, give the presentation to the whole group. The audience should practice active listening and ask appropriate and thoughtful questions.

Teacher Notes:

NAME _____ DATE _____ PERIOD _____

Lesson 7 Review Vocabulary
Equivalent Algebraic Expressions

Use the word cards to define each vocabulary word or phrase.

Word Cards

term	**término**
Definition	**Definición**
each part of an algebraic	cada parte de un expresión
expression separated by a	algebraica separada por un
plus or minus sign	signo más o un signo menos

Circle the terms in the expression below.

$$\boxed{5x} + \boxed{3y} - \boxed{6}$$

Word Cards

coefficient	**coeficiente**
Definition	**Definición**
the numerical factor of a term	el factor numérico de un
that contains a variable	término que contiene una
	variable

Circle the coefficients in the terms below.

$$\boxed{2}z \quad \boxed{7}p \quad \boxed{-10}y$$

Lesson 1 Use Substitution to Solve One-Step Equations

English Learner Instructional Strategy

Vocabulary Support: Frontload Academic Vocabulary

Review *algebraic expression (expresión algebraica)*, *equivalent expression (expresión equivalente)*, *Distributive Property (propiedad distributiva)*, and *evaluate (evaluar)* on the Word Wall.

Write $5(x - 3)$ on the board. Say, *Use the Distributive Property to find an equivalent expression.* Have partners work together. Write the answer on the board: $5(x - 2) = 5x - 10$. Point to the equals sign and ask, *What is this?* **equals sign** Point to both sides of the equals sign and say, *Are these equivalent expressions?* **yes** Say *This is an equation.* Model and prompt students to say, **equation.** Write $x = 6$ next to the equation. Say, *The answer is a solution.* Model and prompt students to say, **solution.**

Write *equals sign (signo de igualdad)*, *equation (ecuación)*, and *solution (solución)* on the Word Wall with math examples.

English Language Development Leveled Activities

Entering/Emerging	Developing/Expanding	Bridging
Word Recognition Have students create a pair of vocabulary cards for the following vocabulary: *constant, variable, equation, equals sign, solution.* On one card they should write the vocabulary word. On the other card, they should put an example of the word. For example, for *constant,* the example card could have the following: $3s + 7$. The 7 can be written in red or circled or otherwise highlighted. Students can use the cards to play a matching game.	**Listen and Respond** Review the terms *equation, constant, variable, solve,* and *solution.* Say, *I will say an equation. You will write it in your notebooks.* Then dictate an equation, such as $y - 3 = 7$. Ask, *What is the variable?* Encourage answers in complete sentences. **The variable is y.** What are the constants? **The constants are 3 and 7.** Say, *Use substitution to solve for y.* Allow some time to solve for y. Ask, *What is the solution?* **The solution is 10.** After you give a few examples, have a student be the "teacher" who dictates an equation and asks questions.	**Share What You Know** Draw the table below. <table><tr><td></td><td>Ana</td><td>Maya</td></tr><tr><td>Round 1</td><td>85</td><td>88</td></tr><tr><td>Round 2</td><td>x</td><td>71</td></tr><tr><td>Round 3</td><td>78</td><td>y</td></tr><tr><td>Total</td><td>234</td><td>233</td></tr></table> Explain that the data shows game scores. Then ask students to write at least two algebraic equations they could use to solve for Ana's and Maya's missing scores. Have partners compare their equations and solutions.

Teacher Notes:

NAME _____ DATE _____ PERIOD _____

Lesson 1 Vocabulary
Use Substitution to Solve One-Step Equations

Use the vocabulary squares to write a definition, a sentence, and an example for each vocabulary word.　Sample answers are given.

equation	Definition a mathematical sentence showing two expressions are equal
Example $3x = 4 + 3; x + 5 = 7; \frac{x}{3} = 7$	Sentence $x + 5 = 7$ is an equation.

equals sign	Definition a symbol of equality
Example $y - 3 = 7$	Sentence All equations contain an equals sign.

solve	Definition to replace a variable with a value that results in a true sentence
Example $3y = 18; y = 6$	Sentence I can solve the equation $3y = 18$ by replacing y with 6.

Lesson 2 One-Step Addition Equations
English Learner Instructional Strategy

Language Structure Support: Tiered Language

Have a volunteer come to the front of the room. Point to the student's shoes and say, *Please* **undo** *your shoelaces.* Ask the class, *Did [student's name] tie or untie the shoes?* **S/he untied the shoes.** Repeat the example for add and subtract. Show students how adding and subtracting can **undo** each other. Say, *Addition and subtraction are inverse operations because they* **undo** *each other.* Write *inverse operations (operaciones inversas)* on the Word Wall.

Write $c + 2 = 5$ on the board. Point to the addition sign and ask, *Is this addition or subtraction?* **addition** *What is the inverse operation?* **subtraction** *Please explain how to solve for c.* **Subtract 2 from each side of the equation.** Repeat with the following examples: $6 = x + 5$ and $3.5 + y = 12.75$.

English Language Development Leveled Activities

Entering/Emerging	Developing/Expanding	Bridging
Manipulatives	**Say and Write**	**Write and Solve**
Use a balance and cubes to model an addition equation. Put five cubes on the left side of the scale and ten cubes on the right. Ask, *Are they equal?* **no** Prompt a student to put cubes on the scales so that it is balanced. *Did you add or subtract?* **add** *How many cubes did you add?* **Five cubes.** *Which side did you add the cubes?* Students can point to the correct side. Extend the activity to writing equations based on the balance model, such as $10 = 5 + x$.	Have students work in pairs. Write a simple addition equation. Have students solve the equation and verbally describe the steps to a partner using vocabulary words. For example, students might say, **[Subtraction] is the inverse operation. [Subtract] _____ from both sides. So, *x* equals _____.**	Have partners work together to write a word problem about money; for example, Nancy went to the pool. She spent $4.50 on admission and $3.75 on snacks. She had $1.75 left. How much money did Nancy start with? Have each pair trade problems with another pair who should make a model, solve the problem, and write step-by-step instructions describing how they found the solution.

Multicultural Teacher Tip

As students work on writing and solving equations, you may notice some ELLs seem to skip steps or write the end result in a different way. This may be due to a strong emphasis on mental math in Mexican and Latin American countries. It is important to model writing each step and encourage students to do the same. Mental math works well in simpler problems, but students may struggle with multi-step problems if they are unfamiliar with the algorithms being taught at this stage.

NAME _____ DATE _____ PERIOD _____

Lesson 2 Vocabulary
One-Step Addition Equations

Use the word cards to define each vocabulary word or phrase and give an
example. **Sample answers are given.**

Word Cards

inverse operations

Definition

operations which undo each

other

Example Sentence

Addition and subtraction are inverse operations; multiplication

and division are inverse operations.

operaciones inversas

Definición

operaciones que se anulan

mutuamente

Word Cards

Subtraction Property of Equality

Definition

If you subtract the same

number from each side of an

equation, they remain equal.

Example Sentence

The Subtraction Property of Equality allows us to subtract the

number 3 from each side of the equation, $x + 3 = 9$.

propiedad de sustracción de la igualdad

Definición

Si sustraes el mismo número de

ambos lados de una ecuación,

siguen siendo iguales.

Lesson 3 One-Step Subtraction Equations
English Learner Instructional Strategy

Vocabulary Support: Cognates

Review *equation (ecaución)*, *solution (solución)*, and *equivalent expressions (expresiones equivalentes)* on the Word Wall. Provide concrete examples to support understanding. Then write and say: *equal, equality, equation, equivalent.* Point out common letters among the words, and discuss how the meanings of these terms are related.

Write *Addition Property of Equality (propiedad de adición de la igualdad), Subtraction Property of Equality (propiedad de sustracción de la igualdad)* on the Word Wall. Write the following frame and have students write two definitions, one for each property: **The _____ Property of Equality: If you [add/subtract] the same number [to/from] each side of the equation, the two sides remain equal.**

English Language Development Leveled Activities

Entering/Emerging	Developing/Expanding	Bridging
Manipulatives	**Say and Write**	**Write and Solve**
Use a balance and cubes to illustrate subtraction equations. Cover the right side of the balance so students don't know how many there are. Put five cubes on the left side of the scale and ten cubes on the right. Ask, *Are they equal?* **no** One at a time, take away cubes from the right side until it is balanced. *Did we add or subtract?* **subtract** *How many cubes did we take away?* **five cubes** *Which side did you take them from?* **right** Extend the activity to writing equations.	Have students work in pairs. Write a simple subtraction equation. Have students solve the equation and verbally describe the steps to a partner using vocabulary words. For example, students might say, **_____ is the inverse operation. Add _____ to both sides. So, *x* equals _____.**	Have partners work together to write another word problem about money; for example, Shiloh went to a movie. He paid $3.25 for admission and bought popcorn for $1.00. He had $5.75 left. How much money did he start with? Have each pair trade problems with another pair who should make a model, solve the problem, and write step-by-step instructions describing how they found the solution.

Multicultural Teacher Tip

Some students may write numbers using slightly different notations. In the U.S., numbers are separated into groups of three place values by commas (3,252,689). In Latin American countries, the groups may be separated by points (3.252.689) or spaces (3 252 689). In Mexico it may be a combination of a comma and apostrophe (3'252,689) or a comma and semicolon (3;252,689). Similarly, some Latin American countries use a comma instead of a decimal point (3,45 as opposed to 3.45).

Lesson 3 Notetaking
One-Step Subtraction Equations

Use Cornell notes to better understand the lesson's concepts. Complete each
sentence by filling in the blanks with the correct word or phrase.

NAME _____ DATE _____ PERIOD _____

Questions	Notes
1. How can I solve a subtraction equation?	I can use _____addition_____ to solve a subtraction equation, because subtraction and _____addition_____ are _____inverse operations_____.
2. What does the Addition Property of Equality say I can do to an equation?	I can _____add_____ the _____same_____ number to each side of an equation and the sides will remain _____equal_____.

Summary

How can the Addition Property of Equality be used to solve subtraction
equations? **See students' work.**

_____

_____

_____

_____

_____

_____

Lesson 4 One-Step Multiplication Equations

English Learner Instructional Strategy

Language Structure Support: Tiered Questions

The teacher should write the equation $3x = 24$ on the board

Entering/Emerging: *Point to the coefficient. What is the coefficient?* **The coefficient is ____.** Repeat with similar questions for *variable, operation,* and *inverse operation.*

Developing/Expanding: *What do you know?* **I know the variable is ____. I know the coefficient is ____.** *How can you find x?* **I can find *x* if I ____.**

Bridging: *Describe how you solved for x.* **I found the coefficient ____. Then I used the ____ Property of Equality and ____ each side by ____.**

English Language Development Leveled Activities

Entering/Emerging	Developing/Expanding	Bridging
Developing Oral Language	**Sentence Frames**	**Role-Play**
On the board, write: $4x = 20$. Then point to the $4x$ and say, *This expression means "4 times the value of x."* Have students chorally say, **4 times the value of *x*.** Solve the equation to find that $x = 5$, point to the 5 and say, *This is the solution.* Prompt the students to say, **The solution is 5.** Now write these expressions: $4t = 16$; $6s = 36$. Point to the expression in each and have students say what it means using this frame: **____ times the value of ____.** Then point to the solution and have students say: **The solution is ____.**	Write: $9f = 45$. Ask, *What kind of equation is this?* **multiplication** Ask, *How can we use division to solve this equation?* Students can respond using these sentence frames: **Divide ____ by ____, and divide ____ by ____. The variable equals ____.** Now write: $\frac{1}{3}h = 3$. Ask, *What kind of equation is this?* **multiplication** *How can we use the reciprocal to solve this equation?* **Multiply both sides by ____. Multiply ____ by ____, and ____ by ____. The variable equals ____.**	Prepare several cards with regular and bargain pricing, such as carrots: 3 for 90¢ or 5 for $1.25. Some of the cards might have no "bargain." A third of the students will be vendors, and the rest will be customers. Give the price cards to the vendors. Customers might say, **Hello. How much for the ____?** Vendor might say: **The price is ____ or ____. How many would you like?** Have customers work together to figure out which is the better price. **____ is the better bargain. I'll take ____, please.**

Multicultural Teacher Tip

ELLs from Vietnam may have a unique way to check their solution to a multiplication problem. For example: $473 \cdot 12 = 5{,}676$. Draw a large X. Add the digits of the top number in the problem $(4 + 7 + 3)$ and write the result (14) at the top of the X. Add the digits of the bottom number $(1 + 2)$ and write the result (3) at the bottom of the X. Multiply the top and bottom numbers of the X $(14 \cdot 3 = 42)$, add the digits of the product $(4 + 2)$ and write the result (6) in the left space of the X. Finally, add the digits of the original answer $(5 + 6 + 7 + 6 = 24)$, add the digits of the result $(2 + 4)$, and write the number (6) in the right space of the X. If the numbers to the left and right of the X match, the answer is correct $(6 = 6$, so 5,676 is correct).

NAME _____ DATE _____ PERIOD _____

Lesson 4 Vocabulary
One-Step Multiplication Equations

Use the definition map to list qualities about the vocabulary word or phrase.
Sample answers are given.

Vocabulary

> ## Division Property of Equality

Characteristics

> You must divide each term by a nonzero number.

Description

> You can divide each side of an equation by the same nonzero number.

> The equation will remain true after the division.

> You can use this property to solve an equation.

$6a = 18$	$15 = 15$	$24 = 8x$
$\dfrac{6a}{6} = \dfrac{18}{6}$	$\dfrac{15}{3} = \dfrac{15}{3}$	$\dfrac{24}{8} = \dfrac{8x}{8}$
$a = 3$	$5 = 5$	$3 = x$

Write and solve example equations.

Course 1 · Module 6 *Equations and Inequalities* **37**

Lesson 5 One-Step Division Equations
English Learner Instructional Strategy

Collaborative Support: Pairwork

Review the *Addition Property of Equality (propiedad de adición de la igualdad)* and *Subtraction Property of Equality (propiedad de sustracción de la igualdad)* from the Word Wall. Have partners review the definitions for each.

Write *Multiplication Property of Equality (propiedad de multiplicación de la igualdad)* and *Division Property of Equality (propiedad de igualdad de la división)*. Have students use the meanings of the Addition and Subtraction Properties of Equality to surmise the meanings of the new properties. Then write the following frame and have students write four definitions, one for each property listed above: **The _____ Property of Equality: If you [multiply/divide by/add/subtract] the same number [on] each side of the equation, the two sides remain equal.** Add the terms to the Word Wall with examples.

English Language Development Leveled Activities

Entering/Emerging	Developing/Expanding	Bridging
Developing Oral Language	**Listen and Write**	**Pairwork**
Write a division equation on the board: $\frac{x}{7} = 4$. Model and prompt statements about the equation. Then, as you say a statement about the equation, students should respond with a complete sentence. For example, if you say, *The variable is x,* then students should say, **Yes, the variable is *x*.** Repeat for several equations. Extend language by suggesting students use more colloquial language, such as, **Hey, that's not right!** or **That's right, you got it!**	Have students listen carefully as you give information about a division equation. For example, say, *The variable is _____. The quotient is _____. The variable is divided by _____.* After you say a statement, have the students repeat it. Then have them write the division equation using the information you supplied. When they have written the equation, have them compare with a partner. If the equations are different, have them discuss the error. If they are the same, have partners solve the equation.	Have students work with a partner. Half of the pairs in the class should write a multiplication word problem that includes a variable. The other half should write a division word problem that includes a variable. Tell students they can reference word problems from this lesson for ideas, if needed. Then have pairs exchange word problems with another set of partners. Ask pairs to solve the problem they have received. Then have both sets of partners meet as a group to check answers.

Teacher Notes:

NAME _____ DATE _____ PERIOD _____

Lesson 5 Notetaking
One-Step Division Equations

Use Cornell notes to better understand the lesson's concepts. Complete each answer by filling in the blanks with the correct word or phrase.

Questions	Notes
1. How can I solve a division equation?	I can use ____multiplication____ to solve a division equation, because division and ____multiplication____ are ____inverse operations____ .
2. What does the Multiplication Property of Equality say I can do to an equation?	I can ____multiply____ each side of an equation by the ____same____ nonzero number, and the sides will remain ____equal____ .

Summary

When solving an equation, why is it necessary to perform the same operation on each side of the equals sign? **See students' work.**

_____

_____

_____

_____

_____

_____

Lesson 6 Inequalities

English Learner Instructional Strategy

Graphic Support: Signal Word Chart

Tell students that there are words in problems that signal inequalities. Write the following list of words and phrases on the board: *over, less than, at least, at most, more than, under, below, above, no more than, no less than, up to.* Have students highlight any of these words or phrases they see in word problems.

Have students create another four-column chart in their math notebooks using *is greater than* (>), *is less than* (<), *is greater than or equal to* (≥), and *is less than or equal to* (≤) as column headings. Have partners work together to determine which word or phrase signals which inequality and write it in the appropriate column. Clarify meanings with examples, if necessary.

Have students include symbols and corresponding phrases on a word wall or anchor chart.

English Language Development Leveled Activities

Entering/Emerging	Developing/Expanding	Bridging
Choral Responses	**Building Oral Language**	**Share What You Know**
Prior to class, prepare a PowerPoint presentation, with one inequality on each slide. Write the inequality symbols >, <, ≥, ≤ on the board and review them. Show the first slide (for example, $a \leq 6$) and then model how to say the inequality. Prompt students to say, *a* **is less than or equal to 6**. Offer both choral and individual practice. Repeat with several other slides until students can confidently name each one.	Write: *You must be over 12 years old to ride the go-karts.* Ask: *Which word signals an inequality?* **over** Have students write an inequality to represent the statement and graph it on a number line. Teach and model cause-and-effect sentences so students can describe their reasoning for how to graph an inequality. Say, *Age (a) is greater than 12, so everything to the right of 12 is shaded.* Model the sentence again and have students repeat it chorally and then individually. Repeat for other examples. Have students use this language as they work through other examples with a partner.	Have a Bridging student work with an Entering/Emerging or Developing/Expanding student as they work on problems involving inequalities. Have them act as the teacher and remind their "students" about how certain words signal an inequality. Encourage language such as, **Remember that *is more than* means "is greater than." This number is greater than _____.** "Teachers" can also assist others in graphing inequalities: It says greater than. Look at the number line. Will the values be to the right or to the left?

Teacher Notes:

NAME _____ DATE _____ PERIOD _____

Lesson 6 Vocabulary

Inequalities

Use the concept web to show examples of inequalities using words and symbols. **Sample answers are given.**

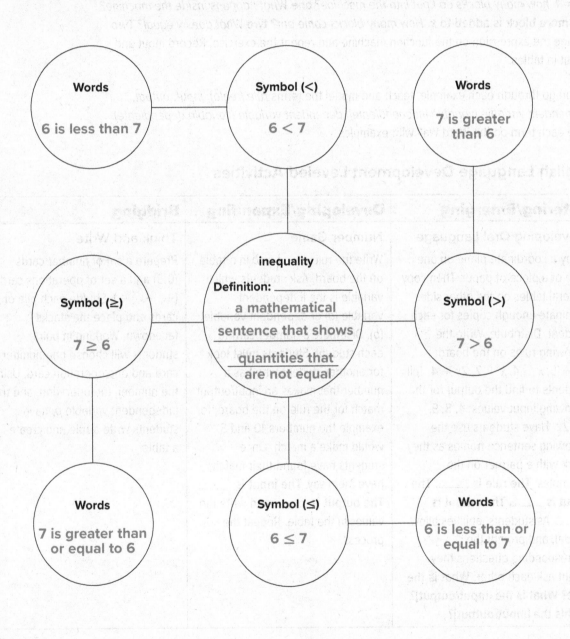

Words

6 is less than 7

Symbol (<)

6 < 7

Words

7 is greater than 6

Symbol (≥)

7 ≥ 6

inequality

Definition: _____
a mathematical
sentence that shows
quantities that
are not equal

Symbol (>)

7 > 6

Words

7 is greater than or equal to 6

Symbol (≤)

6 ≤ 7

Words

6 is less than or equal to 7

Course 1 • Module 6 *Equations and Inequalities* **39**

Lesson 1 Relationships Between Two Variables

English Learner Instructional Strategy

Sensory Support: Input-Output Models and Tables

Use a box to create an input-output machine. Write $x + 1$ on a card and use it to label the machine. Set a bucket of blocks labeled *Input (x)* on one side of the machine. Set an empty bucket labeled *Output (y)* on the other side. Underline *in* and *out* in the words *input* and *output* and say, *We put something IN to the machine, and we get something OUT.* Say, *If x = 1, how many blocks do I put into the machine?* **one** *What happens inside the machine?* **One more block is added to x.** *How many blocks come out?* **two** *What does y equal?* **Two** Change the expression on the function machine and repeat the exercise. Record input and output in tables.

As you go through each example, teach and model the terms *rule (regla), input, output, independent variable (variable independiente), dependent variable (variable dependiente).* Write each term on the Word Wall with examples.

English Language Development Leveled Activities

Entering/Emerging	Developing/Expanding	Bridging
Developing Oral Language	**Number Game**	**Think and Write**
Copy a coordinate plane on one side of a piece of paper. Then copy several tables on the other side. Laminate enough copies for each student. Distribute. Write the following rules on the board: $3x + 5, x - 4, x + 2, 2x + 4$. Tell students to find the output for the following input values: 4, 8, 9, 18, 22. Have students use the following sentence frames as they work with a partner on the examples: **The rule is _____. The input is _____. The output is _____.** As students' abilities allow, model, and prompt the corresponding questions they might ask each other: **What is the rule? What is the [input/output]? Is this the [input/output]?**	Write the rule $a - 7 = b$ in a table on the board. Ask students which variable is the independent variable (a) or dependent variable (b). Distribute a number card to each student. Students must look for another student who has a number that makes an input/output match for the rule on the board; for example the numbers 10 and 3 would make a match. Once students have found their match, have them say, **The input is _____. The output is _____.** and write the values in the table. Repeat the process.	Prepare a set of number cards (0-9) and a set of operations cards ($+, -, \cdot, \div$). Shuffle each pile of cards and place the stacks facedown. Working in pairs, students will choose one number card and one operation card. Using the number, the operation, and the independent variable p, have students write a rule and create a table.

NAME _____ DATE _____ PERIOD _____

Lesson 1 Vocabulary

Relationships Between Two Variables

Use the three-column chart to organize the vocabulary in this lesson. Write the word in Spanish. Then write the definition of each word. Sample answers are given.

English	Spanish	Definition
independent variable	variable independiente	the variable in a function with a value that is subject to choice
dependent variable	variable dependiente	the variable in a relation with a value that depends on the value of the independent variable
input	entrada	the value that replaces the independent variable
output	salida	the resulting value of the dependent variable

Lesson 2 Write Equations to Represent Relationships Represented in Tables

English Learner Instructional Strategy

Graphic Support: Patterns and Tables

Review the word *pattern*. Then write a few number patterns on the board and have students predict what number comes next. Have them use the frame: **The next number in the pattern is ____.** Write a simple equation on the board, such as $y = x + 1$. Point to x and y. Ask, *What are these? Do you know what number this stands for?* Use students' responses to elicit that the letters are *variables*. Say, *x and y are variables.* Repeat the word *variable*, and have students say the word. Write *variable* on the board and underline *vari*. Say, this word part means "change."

Draw an input/output table to depict the equation $y = x + 1$. For each value of x, have students tell the y value, using the frame: **The y value is ____.** Use the table to elicit the terms *dependent* and *independent variable*. Say, *The value of y depends on the value of x. The **dependent variable** is y. The **independent variable** is x.*

English Language Development Leveled Activities

Entering/Emerging	Developing/Expanding	Bridging
Word Knowledge	**Communication Guides**	**Building Oral Language**
Draw an input/output table on the board. Ask, *What is this table called?* **input/output table** *Where is the input?* Students point. Repeat for *output*. Then ask students to identify the dependent and independent variables.	When they understand the math content of a lesson, it is easy for English learners to get away with not using English. When this happens, share a few phrases and sentences students can use to generally discuss what they are practicing. For example, **What answer did you get? My answer is ____. What about yours? How did you get the answer?** Model and prompt appropriate responses, according to the particular math concept students are working on.	Using the content of an input/output table is a great way to practice conditional if...then statements and questions. Draw an input/output table on the board. Model and prompt if...then statements about the content. For example, *If the input is ____, then the output is ____.* Once students have a handle on that, model and prompt the question form of an if...then statement. *If the input is ____, what is the output?*

Teacher Notes:

NAME _____ DATE _____ PERIOD _____

Lesson 2 Notetaking

Write Equations to Represent Relationships Represented in Tables

Use Cornell notes to better understand the lesson's concepts. Complete each part by circling the correct word, or filling in the blanks with the correct word or phrase.

Questions	Notes
1. How can I use an input/output table to write an equation?	An __equation__ can be used to represent the relationship shown in a table. It expresses the __dependent__ variable in terms of the __independent__ variable.

position, p (input, output)	1	2	3	4
value, t (input, output)	5	10	15	20

Questions	Notes
2. In the table, how can I find the output when I know the input?	I can use __repeated__ addition to find the output. __Repeated__ addition is the same as __multiplication__. If the input (p) is 1 and the output (t) is 5, the equation $t =$ __$5p$__ can be used to find the value of the __dependent__ variable, t, for any __independent__ variable, p.

Summary

In the equation $d = 25t$, what is the relationship between the dependent and the independent variables? **See students' work.**

_____

_____

_____

_____

_____

_____

_____

Lesson 3 Graphs of Relationships
English Learner Instructional Strategy

Language Structure Support: Cognates

Write the following vocabulary and cognates: *coordinate plane (plano de coordenadas)*, *ordered pair (par ordenado)*, *graph (gráfica)*, *x-coordinate (coordenada x)*, *y-coordinate (coordenada y)*, *x-axis (eje x)*, *y-axis (eje y)*, and *origin (origen)*. As necessary, model the correct pronunciation and have students repeat the words. The double *o* in *coordinate, the ph* (for /f/) in *graph*, and the *g* (for /j/) in *origin* are potentially troublesome, so spend a couple of minutes going over those. Point out how descriptive words precede the noun they modify, such as *ordered* in *ordered pair*. This contrasts with Spanish, where descriptive words follow the nouns they modify.

English Language Development Leveled Activities

Entering/Emerging	Developing/Expanding	Bridging
Look, Listen, and Identify	**Partners Work/Pairs Share**	**Share What You Know**
Have students write each vocabulary word from the Instructional Strategy above on a sticky note. Display a large coordinate plane, making sure that all of the vocabulary words are represented on the display. As you point to a feature of the plane, such as the origin, have all students hold up the appropriate sticky note from their stack. Then ask individual students, *Label the [origin].* The student should use their sticky note to label the origin. As they do, have students complete the sentence frame, **This is the [origin].**	Give each pair a page with several blank coordinate planes. Review the vocabulary associated with the coordinate plane. Display an input/output table for a simple equation, such as $y = 2x$. Ask partners to complete the table and identify the ordered pairs (*x* and *y* values). Then have them graph the ordered pairs on a coordinate plane. Finally, have them share their resulting graph with another pair and discuss any differences.	Repeat the Developing/Expanding activity. Then have a Bridging student use simple language to describe to an Entering/Emerging student how to find an ordered pair and graph it on a coordinate plane. Then they can act as the "teacher" as their Entering/Emerging partner explains the process in their own words.

Teacher Notes:

NAME _____ DATE _____ PERIOD _____

Lesson 3 Review Vocabulary
Graphs of Relationships

Use the three-column chart to organize the vocabulary in this lesson. Write the
word in Spanish. Then write the definition of each word.

English	Spanish	Definition
coordinate plane	plano de coordenadas	A plane in which a __horizontal__ number line and a __vertical__ number line __intersect__ at their zero points
ordered pair	par ordenado	A pair of numbers used to locate a __point__ on a coordinate plane; written as (x-coordinate, y-coordinate)
graph	gráfica	To place a dot at a point named by an __ordered pair__
x-coordinate	coordenada x	The __first__ number in an ordered pair and relates to a number on the __x__-axis.
y-coordinate	coordenada y	The __second__ number in an ordered pair and relates to a number on the __y__-axis.
origin	origen	The point of __intersection__ of the x-axis and the y-axis on a coordinate plane.

Lesson 4 Multiple Representations

English Learner Instructional Strategy

Vocabulary Support: Support Meaning

Write the following on the board: *$2 per meal, 5 apples for each pie, 10 balls for every player, 18 gifts total*. Point to *per*. Ask, *What does **per** mean?* If students need help, tell them that *per* means "for every" or "each." Tell students when they see *per, each,* or *for every,* then the information tells about *one* item. So, the phrase *$2 per meal* means that you can buy one meal for $2. Check students' understanding by asking questions like, *What does **20 miles per hour** mean?* **20 miles for every hour.** Ask, *What does **total** mean?* **Total means "in all."** Tell students, *When you see the word **total** that is the final answer you are looking for.*

Have students add the new signal words to their signal word charts in their notebooks. *Total* could be a signal word for any operation while *per, for every,* and *each* belong in the *multiplication* category. Tell students to circle these words whenever they see them in a word problem.

English Language Development Leveled Activities

Entering/Emerging	Developing/Expanding	Bridging
Say and Write	**Exploring Language Structure**	**Using Logical Reasoning**
Put "prices" on a few items around the classroom; for example, a book ($9), the trash can ($25), a stapler ($4), and so on. Model and prompt students to say, *$9 per book.* Check choral and individual responses. Write *$9 per book* and have students write it in their notebooks. Continue with other items and their prices. Then replace *per* with *for each* or *for every* and repeat the procedure. You can also replace the word *book* with something else. For a further challenge, ask students to write a rule to represent the cost of some of each item; $c = 9b$ represents the cost c of b books.	Repeat the Entering/Emerging activity. Then teach and model the sentences, *Each book costs $9. Three books cost $27.* Ask students to tell you what the subject of each sentence is (**book, books**). Have students note how the verb changes, depending on whether the subject is singular or plural. Have students write the sentences in their notebooks. Repeat with different numbers of the other classroom examples and their prices.	Have students define the words *dependent* and *independent* in their own words. They should understand that *dependent* means "relies or depends on something else" and that *independent* is the opposite. Have partners look at the following equations and determine which variable is the dependent variable and which is independent: $c = 9b, x + 4 = y$. Then have them tell how they know.

Teacher Notes:

NAME _____ DATE _____ PERIOD _____

Lesson 4 Notetaking
Multiple Representations

Use the definition map to list qualities about the multiple representations of the relationship between two variables. Sample answers are given.

Words

There are 25 pennies
in one quarter.

Define the variables.

p = number of pennies

Write an equation.

$p = 25q$

q = number of quarters

(1, 25)

(2, 50)

(3, 75)

Write three solutions as ordered pairs.

Course 1 · **Module 7** *Relationships Between Two Variables* **43**

Lesson 1 Area of Parallelograms
English Learner Instructional Strategy

Graphic Support: Venn Diagram

Write *polygon, rectangle, parallelogram, rhombus,* and *trapezoid* and the Spanish cognates, *polígono, rectángulo, paralelogramo, rombo,* and *trapezoide,* on the Word Wall. Provide concrete examples for the vocabulary by displaying models for each.

Compare and contrast quadrilateral pairs using a Venn diagram. Have students fill in the similarities between two shapes in the overlapping area and characteristics that are different in the non-overlapping areas. Entering/Emerging students might write a word or a short phrase, but Developing/Expanding and Bridging students should be able to write short sentences. If necessary, display the sentence frames for comparing and contrasting the shapes: **A _____ is like a _____ because _____. A _____ is different from a _____ because _____.** Continue until all quadrilaterals have been compared.

English Language Development Leveled Activities

Entering/Emerging	Developing/Expanding	Bridging
Word Recognition	**Academic Vocabulary**	**Building Oral Language**
Draw several pairs of lines on the board. Some pairs should be parallel, some should intersect, and others should be nonparallel but not intersecting. Write *parallel,* then point to each pair and identify it as parallel or not parallel. Have students chorally repeat **parallel** or **not parallel.** Extend the *l*ls in *parallel* to make them look like a pair of parallel lines. Say, *The two l's are parallel.* Display images of other parallel lines using real world examples (stripes, stair rails, road lines), and have students identify any parallel lines in the images.	Draw a set of parallel lines and a parallelogram, and label them as *parallel* and *parallelogram.* Extend the *l*ls in each word to make them look like pairs of parallel lines, and then identify them as such to reinforce meaning. Draw a rectangle on the board. Point to each set of opposite sides and identify them as parallel. Have students identify the number of pairs of parallel sides in the shape using the frame: **There are _____ pairs of parallel sides in this shape.** Repeat with a square, rectangle, trapezoid, rhombus, and parallelogram.	Have student pairs make a two-column chart labeled *Rectangle* and *Parallelogram.* Ask each pair to cut out a parallelogram and a rectangle from paper or card stock. Say, *Place each shape in the appropriate column.* Display the following sentence frames: **A rectangle and a parallelogram are alike because _____. A rectangle and a parallelogram are different because _____.** Have students use the sentence frames to write sentences comparing and contrasting the two shapes. Ask students to read aloud their sentences.

Multicultural Teacher Tip

Individual praise and recognition may not be as important in some cultures. ELLs from these cultures may be embarrassed or uncomfortable when invited to the board to solve a problem or asked to share an answer with the class. They may be more comfortable during group classroom activities, allowing others in the group to respond in classroom discussions.

NAME _____ DATE _____ PERIOD _____

Lesson 1 Vocabulary
Area of Parallelograms

Use the three-column chart to organize the vocabulary in this lesson. Write the word in Spanish. Then write the definition of each word. Sample answers are given.

English	Spanish	Definition
polygon	polígono	a simple closed figure formed by three or more straight line segments
parallelogram	paralelogramo	a quadrilateral with opposite sides parallel and opposite sides congruent
base base	base	any side of a parallelogram
height height	altura	the shortest distance from the base of a parallelogram to its opposite side
formula $A = bh$	fórmula	an equation that shows the relationship among certain quantities

Lesson 2 Area of Triangles
English Learner Instructional Strategy

Sensory Support: Models

Prepare several parallelograms, including squares, rectangles, and rhombi. Cut one parallelogram diagonally, creating two triangles. Turn and flip the triangles to match them up exactly to its other side. Say, *These are* **congruent** *shapes. They are the same shape. They are the same size.* Model and prompt students to say, **congruent.** Write *congruent* and its Spanish cognate, *congruente,* on the Word Wall with a pictorial example.

Have students cut the rest of the parallelograms diagonally, mix up the triangles, and then work together to match pairs of congruent triangles. As they work, encourage them to use the following language: **These triangles [are/are not] congruent. They [are/are not] congruent because they [are/are not] the same _____ and _____.**

English Language Development Leveled Activities

Entering/Emerging	Developing/Expanding	Bridging
Exploring Language Structure	**Activate Prior Knowledge**	**Number Game**
Display a picture of a tricycle. Say, *This is a tricycle. It has three wheels.* Point to each wheel as you count them. Write *tricycle* and underline the prefix *tri-*. Draw a triangle. Point to each angle as you count them. Say, *This polygon has three sides and three angles. It is called a triangle.* Write *triangle* and underline the prefix *tri-*. Say *triangle* again and have students chorally repeat. Say, *The prefix tri- means "three."* Draw other examples and nonexamples of triangles. Have students give thumbs up if the polygon is a triangle and thumbs down if it is not.	Create a list of triangle dimensions. Then have students work in pairs to draw pictures of several triangles and label the dimensions using your list. Have them determine the area for each and write the following sentence on a separate index card for each triangle: **The area of our triangle is _____.** Put the index cards face up on a desk at the front of the classroom. Have pairs trade triangle drawings with each other and determine the area of each triangle based on the base and height measurements. Finally, have the pairs find the matching index cards to verify their area calculations.	Have students work in pairs. Together, students will make a "puzzle." The pieces of the puzzle are index cards with a base measurement, a height measurement, and a drawing of a triangle with the area clearly displayed. Mix up the cards. Distribute one triangle drawing to each pair, making sure that the drawing is not their own. Have pairs find the index cards with the base and height measurements that equal the given area written on their triangle.

Teacher Notes:

NAME _____ DATE _____ PERIOD _____

Lesson 2 Vocabulary
Area of Triangles

Use the definition to list qualities about the vocabulary word or phrase.
Sample answers are given.

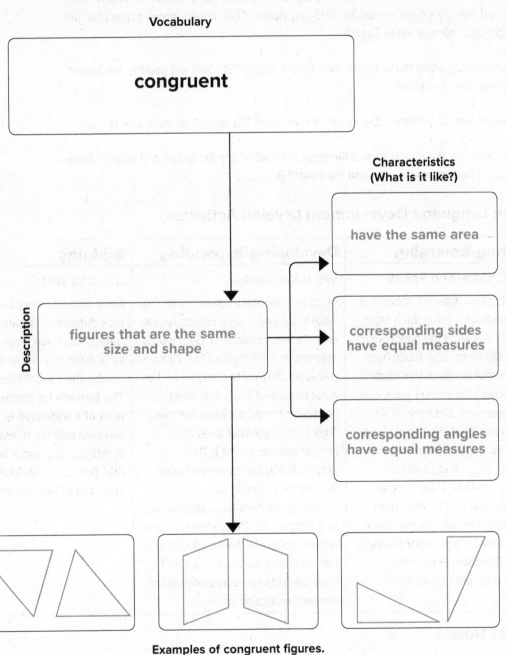

Vocabulary

congruent

**Characteristics
(What is it like?)**

have the same area

Description

figures that are the same
size and shape

corresponding sides
have equal measures

corresponding angles
have equal measures

Examples of congruent figures.

Course 1 · Module 8 *Area* **45**

Lesson 3 Area of Trapezoids

English Learner Instructional Strategy

Language Structure Support: Tiered Language

As you work through any instruction, be sure to check ELLs' understanding during every step. You can do this by asking questions that are appropriate to their level of English acquisition. Assume that Entering/Emerging students can point or say **yes/no**. Your instructions must be very short and clear with known vocabulary. Developing/Expanding students can give short answers and may try simple sentences. Bridging students can create longer sentences and synthesize more information in English.

Entering/Emerging: *Point to the height. What is the height?* Student will point to the height and may only give a number.

Developing/Expanding: *What is the length of base one?* **The length of base one is _____.**

Bridging: *What are the dimensions of the trapezoid? What are the bases and height?* **Base one is _____, base two is _____, and the height is _____.**

English Language Development Leveled Activities

Entering/Emerging	Developing/Expanding	Bridging
Listen, Write, and Speak	**Word Knowledge**	**Say and Write**
Have students draw a trapezoid in their notebooks. Have them listen carefully and label the dimensions as you say them. Say, *Touch base one.* Monitor to check that students are touching the correct base. Say, *Label base one. Base one is 4 inches long.* Students should label b_1 as **4 in.** Repeat the process for base two ($b_2 = 8$ in.) and the height ($h = 4$ in.). Have partners compare their labels. Then have them repeat the dimensions back to you. *What is base one?* **[Base one is] 4 inches.** Repeat the activity with other dimensions.	Write *parallel* and *perpendicular.* Say each word and have students repeat chorally and individually. Both words may cause difficulty for ELLs. Draw a trapezoid. Review that the figure has a set of parallel lines. Ask, *Will these lines ever touch?* **no** *What are these lines called?* **parallel lines** Also review that the height is the perpendicular line between bases. Review the meaning of perpendicular (two lines intersecting at a right angle). Draw examples and nonexamples of a perpendicular line between the trapezoid bases and have students say **perpendicular** or **not perpendicular** for each.	Have students work in pairs as they determine the area of trapezoids. Have them say and write each step of the solution in words, starting with the formula. **The formula for finding the area of a trapezoid is _____. Next we replace b_1 with _____, b_2 with _____, and h with _____. Add the _____. Multiply _____. The area of the trapezoid is _____.**

Teacher Notes:

NAME _____ DATE _____ PERIOD _____

Lesson 3 Review Vocabulary
Area of Trapezoids

Use the concept web to name characteristics of the shape
Sample answers are given.

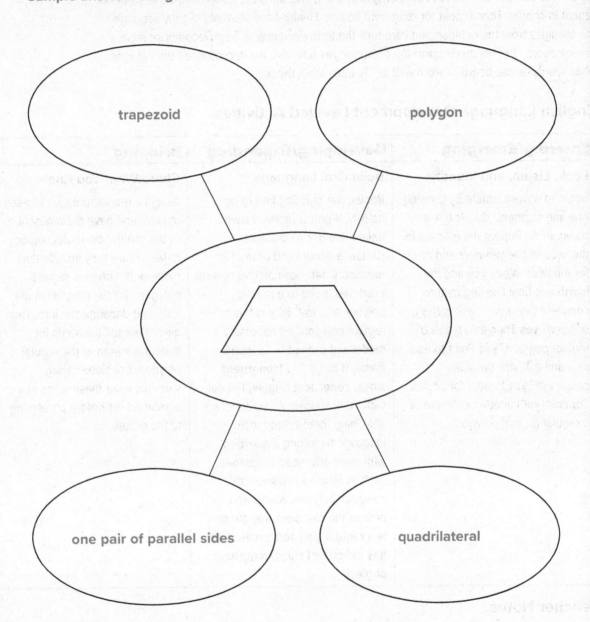

Lesson 4 Area of Regular Polygons
English Learner Instructional Strategy

Sensory Support: Manipulatives

Have pattern blocks available for partners to use to build regular polygons. For example, they should be able to build an octagon with eight triangles. Once they have constructed a given polygon, say the name of the polygon and have students repeat. Introduce or review the term *congruent*. Point to two sides of the polygon and say, *The sides are congruent.* Have students repeat in chorus. Then repeat for congruent angles. Finally, have students slightly separate the triangles from the octagon and introduce the term *decompose*. Say, *Decompose means "break apart." Did we break apart the octagon?* **yes** Say, *Yes, we decomposed the octagon.* Write words on the board or word wall as students learn them.

English Language Development Leveled Activities

Entering/Emerging	Developing/Expanding	Bridging
Look, Listen, and Identify Begin to draw a square by drawing one line segment. Ask, *Is this a polygon?* no Repeat the process for the second line segment and again for the third. When you add the fourth and final line segment to complete the square, ask *Is this a polygon?* **yes** Then ask, *Is this a regular polygon?* **yes** Point to each side and ask, *Are the sides congruent?* **yes** Repeat for angles. Continue with another example of a regular (or not) polygon.	**Build Oral Language** Repeat the Entering/Emerging activity. When students answer, have them use a complete sentence. Model and prompt as necessary. After completing several examples, point to a regular polygon and ask, *Why is this a regular polygon?* As necessary, model and prompt the sentence frame, **It has ____. (congruent sides; congruent angles)** Repeat with other shapes. As students are able, help them extend their language by asking a question with more advanced language, such as *How do you know this is a regular polygon.* Model and prompt the response, **I know this is a regular polygon because (it has congruent sides/congruent angles).**	**Share What You Know** Assign a regular polygon to each student and have them describe to the group how to decompose it. Make sure they include the name of the original regular polygon and the name(s) of the shapes it decomposes into. Then have them tell the steps for finding the area of the regular polygon. Consider having students write these steps in a numbered list before presenting to the group.

Teacher Notes:

NAME _____ DATE _____ PERIOD _____

Lesson 4 Vocabulary
Area of Regular Polygons

Use the three-column chart to organize the vocabulary in this lesson. Write the
word in Spanish. Then write the definition of each word.

English	Spanish	Definition
polygon	polígono	A simple closed figure formed by three or more straight <u>line segments</u>
congruent	congruente	Having the same <u>size</u> and <u>shape</u>
regular polygon	poligono regular	All of the <u>sides</u> are <u>congruent</u> and all of the <u>angles</u> are <u>congruent</u>.
area	área	The measure of <u>surface</u> within a two-dimensional figure
decompose a regular polygon	descomponer una poligono regular	A figure with three <u>sides</u> and three <u>angles</u>

Lesson 5 Polygons on the Coordinate Plane

English Learner Instructional Strategy

Graphic Support: Coordinate Planes

Draw a coordinate plane on the board. Review the following terms (and cognates, if applicable) on the Word Wall: *coordinate plane (plano de coordenadas), origin (origen), x-axis, y-axis, ordered pair (par ordenado), x-coordinate (coordenada x), y-coordinate (coordenada y),* and *graph (gráfica).* Label each item, as applicable. Also review *vertex (vértice).*

Have students use a board marker and an enlarged, laminated coordinate plane to practice plotting points. Write the ordered pairs $A(4, 7)$, $B(8, 7)$, $C(6, 4)$, $D(2, 4)$ on the board. After students have plotted the points, have them use a straightedge and draw $\overline{AB}$, $\overline{BC}$, $\overline{CD}$, and $\overline{DA}$. Tell students that the line above the letters indicates a segment, or a line with a beginning and an end (thus there are no arrows on either end). Ask, *What polygon did you draw?* **parallelogram** Repeat for other polygons. Allow students to use their laminated planes during the lesson.

English Language Development Leveled Activities

Entering/Emerging	Developing/Expanding	Bridging
Developing Oral Language	**Developing Oral Language**	**Making Connections**
Ask each student to draw a polygon on a coordinate plane. They should place all vertices on definable points on the plane. Have one student dictate each ordered pair to a partner, such as **(3, 2).** Then challenge them to connect the points to reproduce each other's shapes on new coordinate planes. Have one student ask, **What shape is it?** and the partner should reply, **It is a _____.**	Ask each student to draw a rectangle on a coordinate plane. They should place vertices on definable points on the plane. Have one student dictate an ordered pair to a partner, using the sentence frame, **The [first/second/third/...] point is located at _____.** Then challenge them to connect the points to reproduce each other's shapes on new coordinate planes. Challenge partners to find the perimeter and area of each rectangle.	Have students think of a real-world scenario in which they would need to know the perimeter of something. Then have them write a problem about the scenario including what they want to do, where they want to do it, and what the problem is. Have them draw a figure with corresponding dimensions on the coordinate plane as an aid. When students have completed writing their problems, have them trade with a partner and solve the partner's problem. Repeat the activity for area.

Teacher Notes:

NAME _____ DATE _____ PERIOD _____

Lesson 5 Review Vocabulary

Polygons on the Coordinate Plane

Use the concept web to identify the parts of the coordinate plane.

Sample answers are given.

Word Bank		
ordered pair	x-axis	y-axis
origin	x-coordinate	y-coordinate

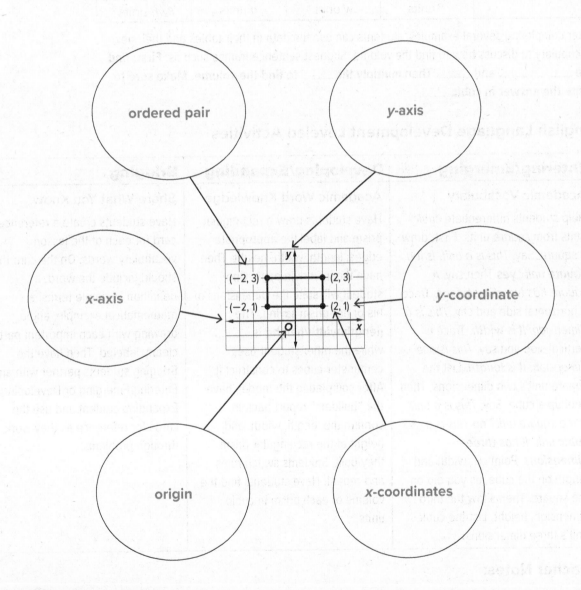

ordered pair

y-axis

x-axis

y-coordinate

origin

x-coordinates

Lesson 1 Volume of Rectangular Prisms

English Learner Instructional Strategy

Graphic Support: Make a Table

Introduce or review the following terms: *three-dimensional figure, rectangular prism, volume,* and *cubic units.* After introducing each word, write the words and their Spanish cognates (*figura tridimensional, prisma rectangular, volumen,* and *unidades cúbicas*) on the Word Wall.

Encourage students to keep track of the dimensions and volume of each rectangular prism they see. Have them use a table like the one below.

Example/Exercise	Length	Width	Height	Volume
	3 ft	2 ft	2 ft	12 ft^3
	ℓ units	w units	h units	ℓwh units^3

After completing several examples, students can use the data in their tables and their new vocabulary to discuss how to find the volume. Suggest sentence frames such as: **First, find the _____, _____, and _____. Then multiply the _____ to find the volume. Make sure to write the answer in cubic _____.**

English Language Development Leveled Activities

Entering/Emerging	Developing/Expanding	Bridging
Academic Vocabulary	**Academic Word Knowledge**	**Share What You Know**
Help students differentiate *cubic* units from *square* units. First, draw a square. Say, *This is a unit. Is it a* **square** *unit?* **yes** Then say, *A square has two* **dimensions**. Trace a horizontal side and say, *This is a dimension. It is* **width**. Trace a vertical side and say, *This is one dimension. It is* **length**. List the square unit's two dimensions. Then hold up a cube. Say, *This is a unit. Is it a square unit?* **no** *This is a* **cubic** *unit. It has* **three dimensions**. Point out width and length on the cube, as you did on the square. Then show the third dimension, height. List the cubic unit's three dimensions.	Have students draw a rectangular prism and label the appropriate edges: length, width, height. Then have them work in pairs. One student will state the dimensions of his or her prism saying, **The [length/width/height] is _____.** while the other student uses centimeter cubes to construct it. After completing the model, have the "builders" report back to confirm the length, width, and height of the rectangular prism they built. Students switch roles and repeat. Have students find the volume of each prism in cubic units.	Have students create a reference card for each of the lesson vocabulary words. On the card they should include the word, a definition in simple terms, a mathematical example, and a drawing with each important part clearly labeled. Then have the Bridging students partner with an Entering/Emerging or Developing/Expanding student and use the cards for reference as they work through problems.

Teacher Notes:

NAME _____ DATE _____ PERIOD _____

Lesson 1 Vocabulary
Volume of Rectangular Prisms

Use the three-column chart to organize the vocabulary in this lesson. Write the word in Spanish. Then write the definition of each word. Sample answers are given.

English	Spanish	Definition
three-dimensional figure	figura tridimensional	a figure with length, width, and height
prism	prisma	a three-dimensional figure with at least three rectangular lateral faces and top and bottom faces parallel
rectangular prism	prisma rectangular	a prism that has rectangular bases
volume	volumen	the amount of space inside a three-dimensional figure
cubic units	unidades cúbicas	used to measure volume; tells the number of cubes of a given size it will take to fill a three-dimensional figure

Lesson 2 Surface Area of Rectangular Prisms
English Learner Instructional Strategy

Collaborative Support: Partners Work/Pairs Check

Have partners work in pairs on problems you assign. Have one student complete the first problem while the second acts as a coach. Then, have students switch roles for the second problem. When they finish the second problem, tell students to get together with another pair and check answers. When both pairs have agreed on the answers, have them continue working in original pairs on the next two problems. After all work has been completed and checked, discuss answers as a class.

English Language Development Leveled Activities

Entering/Emerging	Developing/Expanding	Bridging
Make Connections	**Sentence Frames**	**Number Game**
Display a rectangular prism. Review *length, width,* and *height* and have students point to each. Give each student a copy of a rectangular prism net. Ask, *Is this a net?* **yes** Say, *It is a net for a rectangular prism.* Show an example of a real-life rectangular prism. Have students cut out each face that is represented on the net. Hold up a piece and ask, *Which one is the same size?* Have students match equivalent pieces. Guide students to discover that they can determine surface area of the prism by finding the area of each piece and adding them.	Write: length = 9 in., width = 3 in., height = 2 in. Then say, *These are the dimensions for a rectangular prism.* Have students draw a model of the prism and label its dimensions. Then have them write step-by-step instructions for calculating its surface area. Provide these sentence frames: **This expression shows the area of the prism's top and bottom: _____. This expression shows the area of the prism's front and back: _____. This expression shows the area of the prism's two sides: _____. The sum of the areas is _____ square inches.**	Give a number cube to each pair of students. Introduce game rules: *1) One student rolls the number cube 3 times. The numbers rolled are the dimensions for a rectangular prism. The first number is its length, the second number is its width, and the third number is its height. The student draws the prism and calculates its surface area. 2) The other student takes a turn, repeating the steps in Rule 1. 3) Partners compare surface areas. The student with the greatest surface area scores one point. 4) Partners continue until one student has five points.*

Teacher Notes:

NAME _____ DATE _____ PERIOD _____

Lesson 2 Vocabulary
Surface Area of Rectangular Prisms

Use the definition map to list qualities about the vocabulary word or phrase.
Sample answers are given.

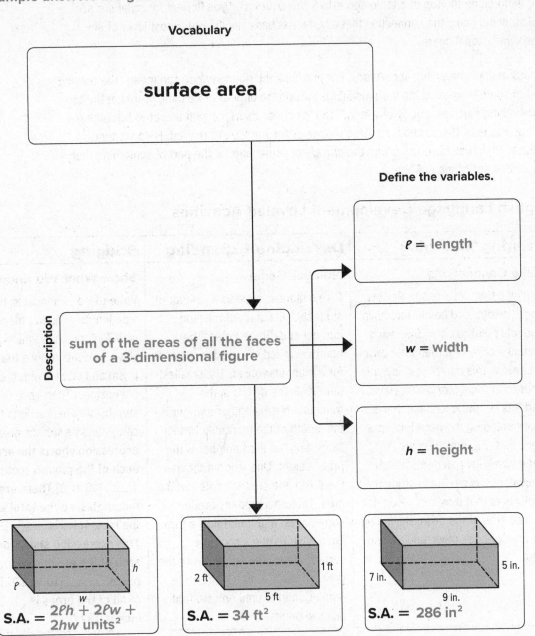

Vocabulary

surface area

Description

sum of the areas of all the faces of a 3-dimensional figure

Define the variables.

ℓ = length

w = width

h = height

S.A. = $2\ell h + 2\ell w + 2hw$ units²

S.A. = 34 ft²

S.A. = 286 in²

Find the surface area of each rectangular prism.

Lesson 3 Surface Area of Triangular Prisms
English Learner Instructional Strategy

Vocabulary Support: Make Connections

Write *surface area* and its Spanish cognate, *área de superficie* on the Word Wall. Introduce the term, and provide a math example. Utilize other translation tools for non-Spanish speaking ELLs. Help students understand that *surface* is the outside area of a figure. Run your hand along the top of a table and ask, *Is this a surface?* **yes** Repeat for other surfaces until students make the connection that a surface is basically the outermost layer of any three-dimensional figure.

Discuss multiple meanings for *surface*. For example, the noun *surface* can mean "the outside layer of something," and the verb meanings include "to appear or become visible at the top of something (such as a body of water)," and "to cover a surface with a coat of something, such as asphalt." Discuss how all these meanings for surface are related. Help students understand that all have to do with the *outside* of something, or the part of something that people can easily see or know.

English Language Development Leveled Activities

Entering/Emerging	Developing/Expanding	Bridging
Make Connections	**Number Game**	**Show What You Know**
Display a triangular prism. Review *length, width,* and *height* and have students point to each. Give each student a copy of a triangular prism net. Ask, *Is this a net?* **yes** Say, *It is a net for a triangular prism.* Have students cut out each face that is represented on the net. Hold up a piece and ask, *Which one is the same size?* Have students match equivalent pieces. Guide students to discover that they can determine surface area of the prism by finding the area of each piece and adding them.	Give a number cube to each pair of students. One student rolls the number cube three times. The numbers rolled are the dimensions for a triangular prism. The smallest number is the height of the triangular base, another number is the length of the triangular base's sides, and the third number is the prism height. One student draws the prism and calculates its surface area. The other student verifies correctness, and then takes a turn. Then have partners compare surface areas. The student with the greatest surface area scores one point. Continue until one student has five points.	Write these dimensions: triangle side length = 10 in., triangle height = 8.7 in., prism height = 8 in. Have students draw a triangular prism and label it with these dimensions. Then have them write step-by-step instructions for calculating its surface area. **This expression shows the area of each of the prism's rectangles: ____. [10 × 8] There are ____ rectangles, so the total area of the rectangles is ____. [3/240 in²] This expression shows the total area of the prism's two triangular bases: ____. [10 × 8.7] The sum of all of the areas is ____ square inches. [327]**

Teacher Notes:

NAME _____ DATE _____ PERIOD _____

Lesson 3 Review Vocabulary
Surface Area of Triangular Prisms

Use the concept web to find the surface area of the triangular prism. Identify the
shape of each face. Find the area of each face. Then find the total surface area.

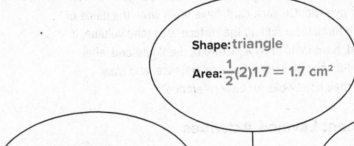

Shape: triangle
Area: $\frac{1}{2}(2)1.7 = 1.7$ cm²

Shape: rectangle
Area: $2(3) = 6$ cm²

Shape: rectangle
Area: $2(3) = 6$ cm²

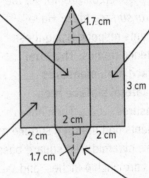

1.7 cm

3 cm

2 cm

2 cm   2 cm

1.7 cm

Shape: rectangle
Area: $2(3) = 6$ cm²

Shape: triangle
Area: $\frac{1}{2}(2)1.7 = 1.7$ cm²

Total Surface Area = $1.7 + 1.7 + 6 + 6 + 6$ or 21.4 cm²

Lesson 4 Surface Area of Pyramids
English Learner Instructional Strategy

Vocabulary Support: Build Background Knowledge

Write the following words and their Spanish cognates, if applicable: *pyramid (pirámide), vertex (vértice), base (base), lateral face,* and *slant height* on the Word Wall. Introduce each term, and provide photos, real-world objects, and math examples to support understanding. Utilize other translation tools for non-Spanish speaking ELLs.

Have students create a card for each three-dimensional figure they know: rectangular prism, triangular prism, pyramid, and triangular pyramid. On each card, have them write the name of the figure, how many faces each has, the formula for finding the surface area (and volume, if applicable). On the other side of the card, have them draw a picture of the figure and label the appropriate parts, such as length, width, height, vertex, base, lateral face, and slant height. Have students keep the cards in their notebooks for easy reference.

English Language Development Leveled Activities

Entering/Emerging	Developing/Expanding	Bridging
Look, Listen, and Identify	**Share What You Know**	**Public Speaking Norms**
Review the meaning of *slant* using photos and real-world objects. Then print these letters: V, W, T, I. Ask, *Which letters have* **slant** *lines?* Have volunteers draw arrows showing the directions of the slant lines on V and W. Then ask, *Which letters have* **vertical** *lines?* Have others draw arrows to show the vertical lines on T and I. Next, draw a pyramid. Label its slant line *slant height,* and label a vertical line from the vertex to the base as *height.* Have students draw and label the slant height and height on other pyramids. Ask them to use one color for the slant height and another for the height.	Ask, *How is the total surface area of a pyramid different from the lateral surface area?* Have students respond using these sentence frames: **The total surface area measures ____. The lateral surface area measures ____.** Then have students find the total surface area of this pyramid: The square base's sides are each 4 inches, and the slant height is 5 inches. Have them explain their solution to an Entering/Emerging level partner.	Show a photo of the Louvre Museum. Have partners research other pyramids in the real-world. Have pairs create a poster with photos of their pyramid and notes about its history. Ask them to draw and label the slant height and height lines on one photo. Then have them present their poster to the class. Encourage language such as, **Today I'd like to tell you about ____. ____ is located in ____. It was built in ____. It was built for (reason).**

Teacher Notes:

NAME _____ DATE _____ PERIOD _____

Lesson 4 Vocabulary
Surface Area of Pyramids

Use the definition map to list qualities about the vocabulary word or phrase.
Sample answers are given.

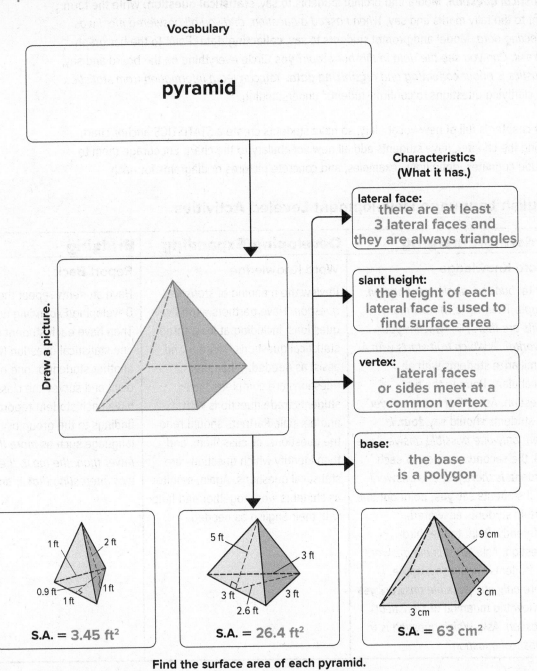

Vocabulary

pyramid

Draw a picture.

**Characteristics
(What it has.)**

lateral face: there are at least 3 lateral faces and they are always triangles

slant height: the height of each lateral face is used to find surface area

vertex: lateral faces or sides meet at a common vertex

base: the base is a polygon

1 ft   2 ft
0.9 ft   1 ft
1 ft

S.A. = 3.45 ft²

5 ft   3 ft
3 ft   3 ft
2.6 ft

S.A. = 26.4 ft²

9 cm
3 cm
3 cm

S.A. = 63 cm²

Find the surface area of each pyramid.

Lesson 1 Statistical Questions

English Learner Instructional Strategy

Graphic Support: Anchor Charts

Write a list of students' native countries on the board. Survey the class with this question: *Which country would you like to visit most?* Tally students' responses and create a bar graph to depict survey results. Underline the question on the board and say, *This question is a statistical question.* Model and prompt students to say, **statistical question.** Write the term. Point to the tally marks and say, *When I asked a question, and you all answered me, I was collecting data.* Model and prompt students to say, **collecting data.** Point to the bar graph and ask, *Can you see the data in this bar graph?* **yes** Circle everything on the board and say, *Statistics is about **collecting** and **organizing data.** You can learn information from statistics.* Ask clarifying questions to confirm students' understanding.

This chapter is full of new vocabulary, so have students create a STATISTICS anchor chart. During the chapter, have students add all new vocabulary to the chart. Encourage them to include cognates, definitions, examples, and concrete pictures or diagrams for each.

English Language Development Leveled Activities

Entering/Emerging	Developing/Expanding	Bridging
Word Knowledge	**Word Knowledge**	**Report Back**
Write: *banana, apple, watermelon, grape.* Then write: 1) *How many fruits are there?* 2) *Which is your favorite?* 3) *Which fruit starts with A?* Familiarize students with all vocabulary. Point to the first question. Ask, *What is the answer?* All students should say, **four.** *Is there only one possible answer?* **yes** Ask the second question to each student. *Is there just one answer?* **no** If students say **yes,** point out that certain students answered differently. Point to the third question. Ask, *What is the answer?* All students should say, **apple.** *Is there only one possible answer?* **yes** Review the meaning of *statistical question.* Ask, *Which question is a statistical question?*	Review the meaning of *statistical question.* Have partners write five questions, including at least three statistical questions. Monitor and assist as needed. When their questions are complete, have students trade questions with another pair. Partners should read the questions, discuss them, and then identify which questions are statistical questions. Again, monitor as students work together and help with their English as needed.	Have students repeat the Developing/Expanding activity. Then have each student choose one statistical question (written by another student or one of their own) and survey the class. Then have each student report their findings to the group using language such as *more than, fewer than, the most, the least, it was interesting that...,* and so on.

Teacher Notes:

NAME _____ DATE _____ PERIOD _____

Lesson 1 Vocabulary
Statistical Questions

Use the three-column chart to organize the vocabulary and key words in this
lesson. Write the word in Spanish. Then write the definition of each word.

English	Spanish	Definition
statistics	la estadística	collecting, organizing, and interpreting data
collect	recoger	to gather data together
organize	organizar	to put in order
interpret	interpretar	to tell the meaning of data
data	data	pieces of information that are gathered for statistical purposes
statistical question	pregunta estadística	a question that has a variety of possible answers

Lesson 2 Dot Plots and Histograms
English Learner Instructional Strategy

Vocabulary Support: Visual Examples

Use a simple example of collected data. Draw a bar graph to represent the data. Ask, What is this? **bar graph** Point out the information represented along the horizontal axis and the meaning of the numbers on the vertical line. Use other data to create a **dot plot.**

Ask each student in the class what their birth month is. Write their information in a table. Point to the list of months and say, This is a long list. Let's combine some months. Draw a histogram. Label the vertical line from 0 to 10. Along the horizontal line, write: *Jan–Mar, Apr–June, July–Sep, Oct–Dec.* Draw a bar on the histogram to represent the number of students born in that span (the frequency). Point to the histogram and say, *This is a* **histogram.** Model and prompt students to say the word.

Point out the similarities between the bar graph, the dot plot, and the histogram. The main difference is that the histogram uses a range of values (intervals) on the horizontal line of the graph.

English Language Development Leveled Activities

Entering/Emerging	Developing/Expanding	Bridging
Look and Identify	**Look and Say**	**Show What You Know**
Prepare several different dot plots, bar graphs, and histograms to show students. Post the displays on the board or on the walls around the room. Students should point to the histograms. Practice the sentence frame, **This [is/is not] a histogram.** Repeat for *dot plot.* Have students find a partner and go to each statistical display and tell whether it is a histogram or a dot plot. If students disagree, help them determine who is correct by pointing out the characteristics of a histogram.	Repeat the Entering/Emerging activity. Once students have correctly determined which displays are histograms, have them identify the intervals on each one. Have them use the following frame to report: **The interval is ____ to ____.** Then have them look at the frequency for each interval and report on it: **The frequency for interval ____ is ____.** Finally, ask students how they could determine the best intervals to use for different sets of data.	Have partners discuss the differences between a dot plot and a histogram. Ask, *Why is one better to use than another? In what situations should a histogram be used? The dot plot?* Then have partners write an example of data that could be represented in a histogram or dot plot. Challenge them to create a real-world problem using the data. Once they are finished, have them trade problems and data with another pair who will then create a histogram or dot plot based on the information and the data.

Teacher Notes:

NAME _____ DATE _____ PERIOD _____

Lesson 2 Vocabulary
Dot Plots and Histograms

Use the vocabulary squares to write a definition, a sentence, and an example for each vocabulary word.

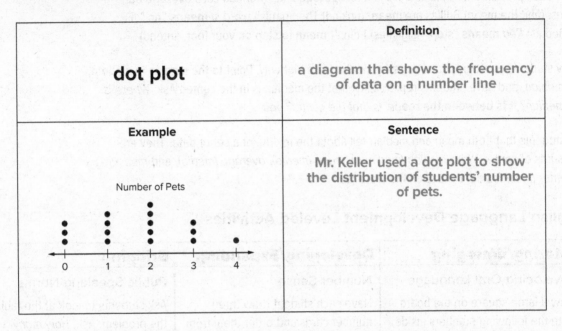

dot plot	**Definition** a diagram that shows the frequency of data on a number line
Example Number of Pets	**Sentence** Mr. Keller used a dot plot to show the distribution of students' number of pets.

histogram	**Definition** a type of bar graph used to display numerical data organized into equal intervals
Example Test Scores	**Sentence** The test scores were displayed in a histogram with intervals of ten points.

Lesson 3 Measures of Center
English Learner Instructional Strategy

Vocabulary Support: Word Wall

Write: *I like to swim, but I am not fast. I am an* **average** *swimmer.* Underline *average*, and ask if anyone can guess what it means. In this case, it means "in the middle" or "not the best and not the worst." Use the same method to introduce other meanings of *average* and *mean*. Some example sentences include: *It's just an* **average** *bike.* (normal) *Let's* **average** *our scores.* (find the mean) *Bullies are* **mean**. (unkind) *The Spanish word sí* **means** *"no."* (is defined as) *Red* **means** *"stop."* (signifies) *I didn't* **mean** *to step on your foot.* (intend)

Show students photographs of a grassy median on a highway. Point to the median in a photo, say *median,* and have students repeat. Elicit that the median is in the center. Ask, *Where is the median?* **It is between the roads.** *Is that the center?* **yes**

Tell students that both mean and median tell about the middle of a set of data. They are measures of center. Write *median (mediana), mean (medio), average (medio),* and *measures of center (medidas del centro)* on the Word Wall.

English Language Development Leveled Activities

Entering/Emerging	Developing/Expanding	Bridging
Developing Oral Language	**Number Sense**	**Public Speaking Norms**
Draw a large square on the board. Write the following numbers inside the box: 3, 5, 7, 3, 4, 8, 9, 2, 3, 6, 5. Say, *Order the numbers from smallest to largest.* The correct order is: 2, 3, 3, 3, 4, 5, 5, 6, 7, 8, 9. Point to a number and ask, *Is this the median, or middle number?* Model how to mark off one number from each end of the list to find the median. Prompt students to say, **The median is 5.** Help students calculate the mean and then prompt them to say, **The mean is 5.**	Have each student draw three number cards and order them from least to greatest. (If the same numbers are drawn, put them beside each other.) Then have students combine cards with a partner and order the cards again. Encourage them to use *greater than, less than and equal to* to compare numbers. Have two pairs of students combine and order their cards. (There should now be 12 cards in the group.) Ask each group to find the mean, median, and mode of their set.	Ask students to look at the table in the problem. Ask, *How many pieces of data (values) are in the table?* Some students may consider the 0 to be a non-value. Lead a "debate" about why the 0 value should be counted as a piece of data. Encourage students to use language such as, **It should be counted because _____. I agree. I don't agree. If _____, then _____.**

Teacher Notes:

NAME _____ DATE _____ PERIOD _____

Lesson 3 Vocabulary
Measures of Center

Use Cornell notes to better understand the lesson's concepts. Complete each sentence by filling in the blanks with the correct word, number, or phrase.

Questions	Notes
1. What are the different measures of center?	Measures of center are numbers that describe the _____center_____ of a numerical data set. The mean of a data set is the ___sum___ of the data divided by the number of __pieces of data__. It is also called the _____average_____. The median of a data set is the _____middle_____ value when the pieces of data are arranged ___in order___.
2. How can I calculate the mean?	Example: The points scored by 5 players in a basketball game were 15, 7, 15, 19, 4. I can ___add___ the scores and then ___divide___ by 5. $15 + 7 + 15 + 19 + 4 =$ __60__ $\frac{60}{5} =$ __12__
3. How can I calculate the median?	Example: The points scored by 5 players in a basketball game were 15, 7, 15, 19, 4. I can put the numbers in ___order___: 4, 7, 15, 15, 19. The middle value is __15__

Summary
How does the measure of center help me analyze a data set? **See students' work.**

Lesson 4 Interquartile Range and Box Plots
English Learner Instructional Strategy

Vocabulary Support: Frontload Academic Vocabulary

Have students place 11 counters in a row. Model as you say, *Put a finger on the counter at the far left. Now put a finger on the counter at the far right.* Gesture to the entire set from left to right and say, *This is the* **range.** Say, *Put your finger on the middle counter.* Model how students should slide it upward. Point to the middle counter and say, *This is the* **median.** Point to smaller groups to the left of the median and ask, *Where is the middle counter of this group?* Model sliding it downward. Say, *This is the* **first quartile.** Repeat for the **third quartile** of the other small group. Gesture to the distance from the first to the third quartile and say, *This is the* **interquartile range.** Check students' understanding until firm. Write the lesson vocabulary (and Spanish cognates, if applicable) on the Word Wall or anchor chart with examples.

English Language Development Leveled Activities

Entering/Emerging	Developing/Expanding	Bridging
Word Knowledge	**Developing Oral Language**	**Building Oral Language**
Have students write each of these words on its own sticky note: *range, median, first quartile, third quartile, interquartile range.* Write these ordered numbers on the board: 0, 8, 11, 13, 13, 15, 16, 16, 17, 17, 17, 18, 18, 20, 20. Draw a bracket above the set, ranging from 0 all the way to 20. Draw a bracket below the set, ranging from the first 13 to the first 18. Have students, one at a time, use a sticky note to label a part of the set of numbers. Remove notes and repeat until all students have participated. If possible, have students use a sentence as they label each term: **This is the _____.**	Arrange students in a line by height. Have them take turns measuring their heights in inches and recording them in a table. Next, have students determine the range, median, first quartile, third quartile, and interquartile range. As students work through the activity, have them use language such as **Let's find the _____. This is the middle number. The [median/range/ etc.] is _____.**	Have students think about and discuss all of the different measures of variation. How many can they name? Assign one of the following words to each student: *first quartile, third quartile, interquartile range, range.* Have students explain how to find their assigned measure to the others; encourage them to model using manipulatives and have their "students" follow along with their own manipulatives. Students may write out the directions first, if they choose.

Teacher Notes:

Student page

Lesson 4 Vocabulary
Interquartile Range and Box Plots

Use the three-column chart to organize the vocabulary and key words in this lesson. Write the word in Spanish. Then write the definition of each word.

English	Spanish	Definition
measures of variation	medidas de variación	A measure used to describe the __distribution__ of data
quartiles	cuartiles	Values that divide a data set into __four__ equal parts
first quartile	primer cuartil	For a data set with the median *M*, the first quartile is the median of the data values __less__ than *M*.
third quartile	tercer cuartil	For a data set with the median *M*, the third quartile is the median of the data values __greater__ than *M*.
interquartile range	rango intercuartil	A measure of variation in a set of numerical data; the distance between the __first__ and __third__ quartiles of the data set
range	rango	The __difference__ between the greatest number and the least number in a data set

56 Course 1 · Module 10 *Statistical Measures and Displays*

Course 1 · Module 10 *Statistical Measures and Displays* 56

Copyright © McGraw-Hill Education.

Lesson 5 Mean Absolute Deviation
English Learner Instructional Strategy

Sensory Support: Realia

Write *mean absolute deviation* and its Spanish cognate, *desviación media absoluta,* on the Word Wall. Briefly introduce the meaning of the term, and then, during the lesson, frequently refer to the Word Wall to reinforce meaning and to provide concrete examples.

Organize students into several small groups. Direct each group to create a table listing the total number of pages for each chapter in one of their textbooks. Then say, *Find the mean absolute deviation for the data.* Give students time to complete the task. Then display the following sentence frames to help students share the data: **The mean number of pages per chapter is _____. The mean absolute deviation is _____.** If groups attained different results, have students compare data and methods to see why.

English Language Development Leveled Activities

Entering/Emerging	Developing/Expanding	Bridging
Review Vocabulary Create a number line on the board. Mark 0 at the the midpoint. Review the idea of absolute value. Create a set of sticky notes from −20 to 20 and distribute to students. Have them put the numbers on the number line. Call out a number. Ask, *What is the absolute value of _____?* If students need help, remind them to count from the number to zero, then state the value.	**Choral Responses** Have students write their full names (first, middle, and last) on whiteboards and say, **My name is _____.** Use the names to create a set of data showing how many letters each name contains. Model finding the mean absolute deviation of the data. As you work, narrate the steps and have students chorally repeat key vocabulary, such as: *mean, absolute, value, average, difference,* and *mean absolute deviation.* Say each word slowly and precisely to model correct pronunciation.	**Turn & Talk** Ask, *How do outliers affect the mean average deviation? Without the outlier, would the mean absolute deviation be greater, lesser, or the same? How do you know?* Have students turn to another student and discuss the answer. After students have had time to think about the question, lead a discussion and provide data that shows that when there are outliers, the sum of the distances from the mean would increase. This would cause the mean absolute deviation to be greater.

Teacher Notes:

NAME _____ DATE _____ PERIOD _____

Lesson 5 Notetaking
Mean Absolute Deviation

Use Cornell notes to better understand the lesson's concepts. Complete each sentence by filling in the blanks with the correct word or phrase.

Questions	Notes
1. How do I find the mean absolute deviations for a data set?	I find the _____ **sum** _____ of the distances between each data value and the _____ **mean** _____, then I _____ **divide** _____ by the number of data values.
2. How do I compare mean absolute deviations for two data sets?	The data set with a _____ **smaller** _____ mean absolute deviation has data values that are _____ **closer** _____ to the mean than a data set with a _____ **greater** _____ mean absolute deviation.

Summary

What does the mean absolute deviation tell you about a set of data?

_____ See students' work. _____

_____

_____

_____

_____

Lesson 6 Outliers

English Learner Instructional Strategy

Collaborative Support: Hands-On Math Games

Give each pair of students a stack of sticky notes, paper, and pencil. Have them determine a team name. Dictate the following numbers, one per sticky note: 25, 30, 180, 40, 25, 35, 40, 25, 30, 25. Pose a question (see suggestions below) and have teams find the answer. When they think they know, they should say their team name. Entering/Emerging students may point to the answer or say one word, but Developing/Expanding and Bridging students should use complete sentences. If the answer is correct, the team receives a point. Before moving on to the next instruction, make sure all students understand the answers.

Vary your questions. For example, *Put the numbers in order. Show me the _____. Point to the _____. What is the _____? Tell me the _____. Is there a(n) _____?* (Follow-up: *What is it?*) Ask students to show each of the following for a point: range, mode, median, mean, interquartile range, first quartile, third quartile, outlier, and mean absolute deviation. You might offer extra points for some of the more difficult-to-determine measures. You may require that Bridging students assist Entering/Emerging students attempts to answer for their team, or a team must explain how they found the answer in order to receive the point.

English Language Development Leveled Activities

Entering/Emerging	Developing/Expanding	Bridging
Word Knowledge	**Public Speaking Norms**	**Turn & Talk**
Draw several examples of outliers; for example, draw a dot plot with several points and at least one outlier, or write a list of numbers with an outlier. Point to the outlier on the dot plot. Say, *This point lies outside the group of numbers. It is an **outlier**.* Repeat *outlier* and have students repeat. Write the word on the board. Then introduce the following words or phrases that can be used to describe the outlier: *outside, far away from, much greater/less than.* Ask questions such as, *Is an outlier far away from the other points?* **yes**	Teach useful "question language" students can use when they need to ask for help, such as: **Excuse me. Can you help me? I don't understand _____. What does this word mean? Is this correct? What did I do wrong? I still don't understand.** Also teach them the niceties of thanking someone for their help: **Okay, Thanks! Wow, that was easy. Thank you for your help. You were really helpful. You explained that well. I understand now.**	Have students turn to another student and discuss the answer to the following question: *If a data set has an outlier, why might you use the median instead of the mean?* After students have had time to think about the question, discuss the question as a group. Then ask another question for partners to discuss: *What happens to the mean, median, and mode when there is an outlier?*

Teacher Notes:

NAME _____ DATE _____ PERIOD _____

Lesson 6 Vocabulary
Outliers

Use the definition map to list qualities about the vocabulary word or phrase.
Sample answers are given.

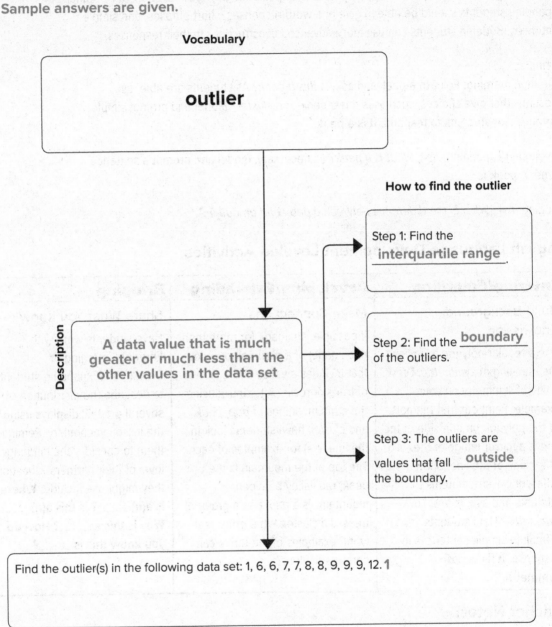

Vocabulary

outlier

How to find the outlier

Step 1: Find the
__interquartile range__.

Description

A data value that is much
greater or much less than the
other values in the data set

Step 2: Find the __boundary__
of the outliers.

Step 3: The outliers are
values that fall __outside__
the boundary.

Find the outlier(s) in the following data set: 1, 6, 6, 7, 7, 8, 8, 9, 9, 9, 12. **1**

Example

Lesson 7 Interpret Graphic Displays
English Learner Instructional Strategy

Language Structure Support: Tiered Questions

Take some time to introduce the lesson vocabulary using visual displays. Then ask tiered questions to English learners to evaluate their understanding of the vocabulary. Remember that Entering/Emerging students may only be able to point and say "yes" or "no." Developing/Expanding students should be able to give one-word responses, short phrases, and simple sentences. Bridging students can use more advanced constructions in their responses.

Examples

Entering/Emerging: Point to a peak and ask, *Is this a peak?* As students are able, ask questions that give choices, such as *Is this a peak or a cluster?* Model and prompt simple sentences for students to respond: **It is a peak.**

Developing/Expanding: Ask, *What is a peak?* As necessary, model and prompt a sentence frame: **A peak is _____.**

Bridging: Ask, *What is the difference between a peak and an outlier?*

English Language Development Leveled Activities

Entering/Emerging	Developing/Expanding	Bridging
Build Background Knowledge	**Make Connections**	**Share What You Know**
Use a regular polygon to review the meaning of *symmetric*. Draw a line of symmetry on your example. Point out that the part of the polygon on one side of the line is a mirror image of the other side of the line. Show different classroom items to students and ask, *Is this symmetric?* Help students formulate simple sentences in response: **It [is/is not] symmetric.**	If possible, an image (or more than one image) of a mountainous view that includes a valley and a cluster of trees or rocks. After introducing the math meanings of *gap, peak,* and *cluster,* have students look in the image(s) for examples of each. The top of the mountain is the peak, the valley between mountains is a gap, and a group of trees is a cluster. What other real-world examples of the terms can partners think of?	Have students work with Entering/Emerging or Developing/Expanding students to describe the distribution of several graphic displays using the lesson vocabulary. Remind them to consider the language level of their partners. Questions they might use include: **Where is a(n) _____? Is this a(n) _____? Why is this a _____? How do you know this is _____?**

Teacher Notes:

Student page

NAME _____ DATE _____ PERIOD _____

Lesson 7 Vocabulary
Interpret Graphic Displays

Label each feature on the histogram with the correct word from the word bank.
Then define the word in your own words.

Word Bank		
cluster	gap	peak

Vocabulary word: ____peak____
Definition: ___the most frequently___
__occurring value or interval of__
__values in a set of data__

Vocabulary word: ____gap____
Definition: ___an area in a set of___
__data where there are no data__
__values__

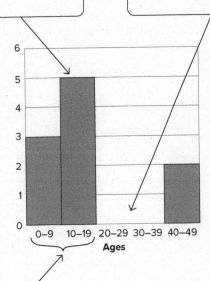

Vocabulary word: ____cluster____
Definition: ___where data values___
__are grouped closely together__

_____

Dinah Zike Explaining
Visual Kinesthetic Vocabulary®, or VKVs®

What are VKVs and who needs them?

" VKVs are flashcards that animate words by kinesthetically focusing on their structure, use, and meaning. VKVs are beneficial not only to students learning the specialized vocabulary of a content area, but also to students learning the vocabulary of a second language. "

Dinah Zike | Educational Consultant

Dinah-Might Activities, Inc. – San Antonio, Texas

Why did you invent VKVs?

" Twenty years ago, I began designing flashcards that would accomplish the same thing with academic vocabulary and cognates that Foldables® do with general information, concepts, and ideas—make them a visual, kinesthetic, and memorable experience. "

Dinah Zike's
Visual
Kinesthetic
Vocabulary

I had three goals in mind:

- **Making two-dimensional flashcards three-dimensional**

- **Designing flashcards that allow one or more parts of a word or phrase to be manipulated and changed to form numerous terms based upon a commonality**

- **Using one sheet or strip of paper to make purposefully shaped flashcards that were neither glued nor stapled, but could be folded to the same height, making them easy to stack and store**

Why are VKVs important in today's classroom?

" At the beginning of this century, research and reports indicated the importance of vocabulary to overall academic achievement. This research resulted in a more comprehensive teaching of academic vocabulary and a focus on the use of cognates to help students learn a second language. Teachers know the importance of using a variety of strategies to teach vocabulary to a diverse population of students. VKVs function as one of those strategies. "

How are VKVs used to teach content vocabulary to EL students?

" VKVs can be used to show the similarities between cognates in Spanish and English. For example, by folding and unfolding specially designed VKVs, students can experience English terms in one color and Spanish in a second color on the same flashcard while noting the similarities in their roots. "

What organization and usage hints would you give teachers using VKVs?

" Cut off the flap of a 6" x 9" envelope and slightly widen the envelope's opening by cutting away a shallow V or half circle on one side only. Glue the non-cut side of the envelope into the front or back of student workbooks or journals. VKVs can be stored in this pocket.

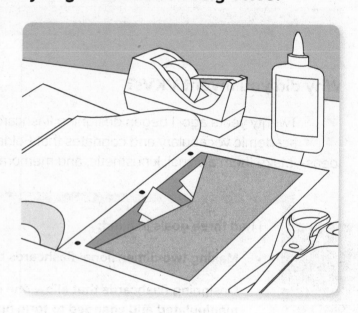

Encourage students to individualize their flashcards by writing notes, sketching diagrams, recording examples, forming plurals (radius: radii or radiuses), and noting when the math terms presented are homophones (sine/sign) or contain root words or combining forms (kilo-, milli-, tri-).

As students make and use the flashcards included in this text, they will learn how to design their own VKVs. Provide time for students to design, create, and share their flashcards with classmates. "

Dinah Zike's book Foldables, Notebook Foldables, & VKVs for Spelling and Vocabulary 4th-12th won a Teachers' Choice Award in 2011 for "instructional value, ease of use, quality, and innovation"; it has become a popular methods resource for teaching and learning vocabulary.

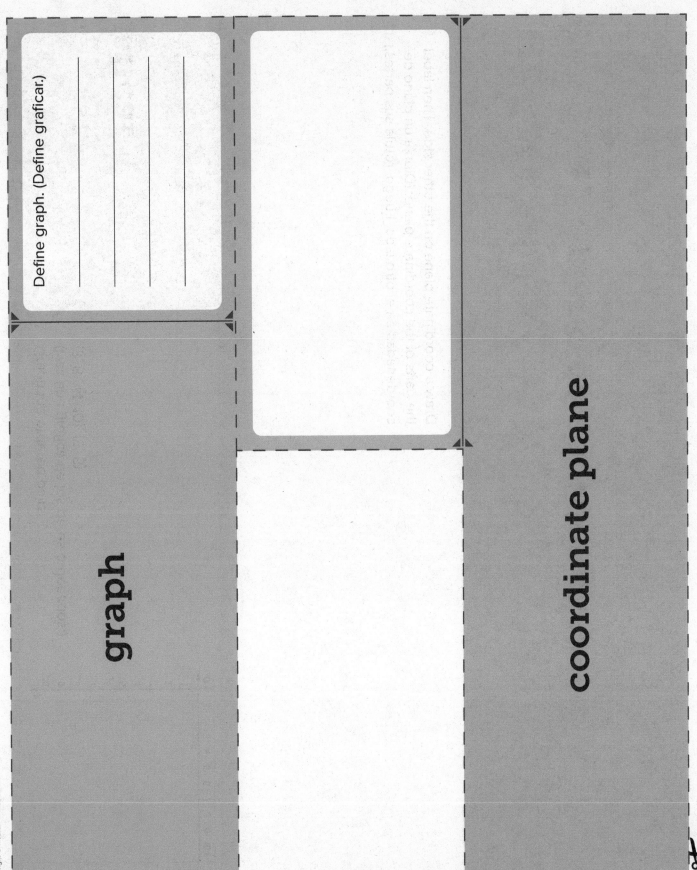

Define graph. (Define graficar.)

graph

coordinate plane

Dinah Zike's
Visual
Kinesthetic
Vocabulary

VKV

✂ cut on all dashed lines

◤ fold on all solid lines ◢

aficar

Graph the ordered pairs.
(Haz una gráfica de los pares ordenados.)
(3, 8), (4, 10), (5, 5)

Draw a coordinate plane on the other side. Then label the parts of the coordinate plane. (Dibuja un plano de coordenadas en el otro lado. Luego, rotula sus partes.)

plano de coordenadas

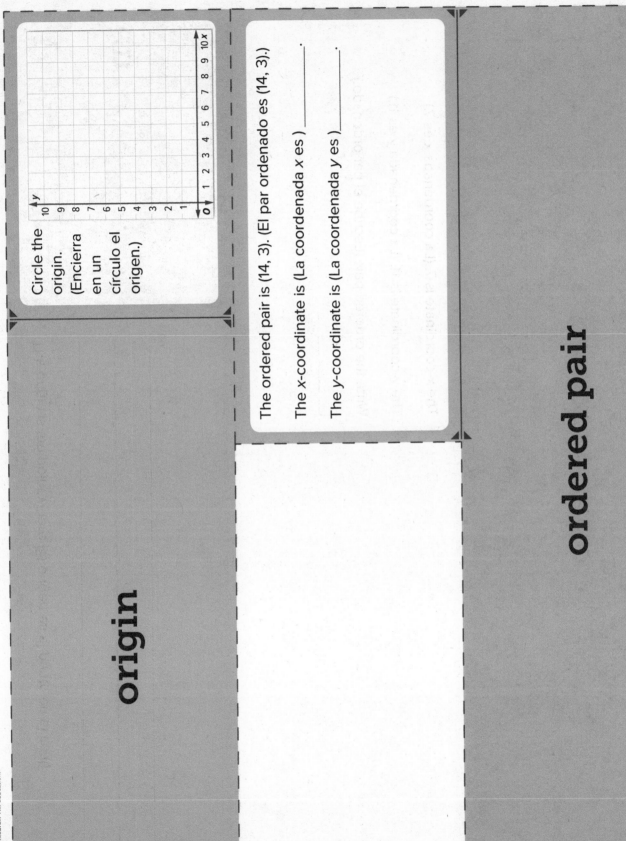

Circle the origin. (Encierra en un círculo el origen.)

The ordered pair is (14, 3). (El par ordenado es (14, 3).)

The x-coordinate is (La coordenada x es) _____ .

The y-coordinate is (La coordenada y es) _____ .

origin

ordered pair

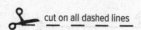
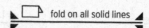
en

par ordenado

The x-coordinate is 7. (La coordenada x es 7.)

The y-coordinate is 11. (La coordenada y es 11.)

Write the ordered pair. (Escribe el par ordenado.)

(_____ , _____)

The origin is the point where (El origen es el punto en el cual) cut on all dashed lines

fold on all solid lines

Define unit price.
(Define precio unitario.)

____

____

____

____

unit price

Circle the greater unit price. (Encierra en un círculo el mayor precio unitario.)

6 tickets for $84

5 tickets for $75

x

Circle the *y*-coordinates (Encierra en un círculo las coordenadas *y*.)

(4, 18)	(23, 12)
(5.9, 65)	(0.9, 12.1)

***y* -coordinate**

Dinah Zike's
Visual
Kinesthetic
Vocabulary

✂ cut on all dashed lines

📄 fold on all solid lines

unitario

coordinada-*y*

x

Five chairs cost $110. Find the unit price. (Cinco sillas cuestan $110. Halla el precio unitario.)

_____

Circle the *x*-coordinates (Encierra en un círculo las coordenadas *x*.)

(4, 18)   (23, 12)   (0.9, 12.1)

(5.9, 65)

precio

List 3 different forms of rational numbers. (Enumera tres formas de representar los números racionales.)

rational number

Write each number as a fraction (Escribe los números como fracciones.)

12 = _____

0.35 = _____

3.1 = _____

Dinah Zike's
Visual
Kinesthetic
Vocabulary

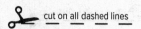
cut on all dashed lines

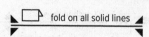
fold on all solid lines

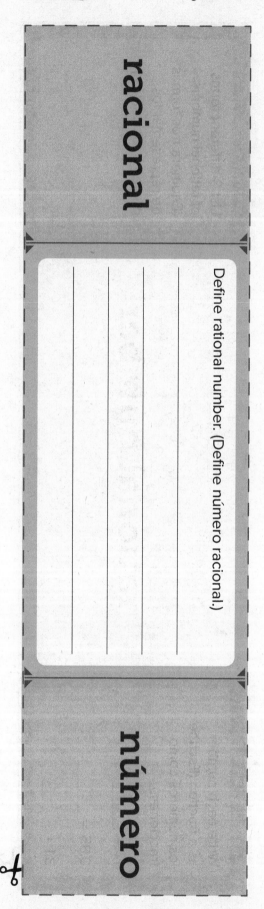

racional

Define rational number. (Define número racional.)

número

Circle the word that is related to the Commutative Property. (Encierra en un círculo la palabra que se relaciona con la propiedad conmutativa.)

grouping   order

To solve $8 \div \frac{3}{4}$, multiply _____ by the reciprocal of _____. (Para resolver $8 \div \frac{3}{4}$, multiplica _____ por el recíproco de _____.)

Commutative Property

Define Commutative Property. (Define propiedad conmutativa.)

reciprocal

Dinah Zike's
Visual
Kinesthetic
Vocabulary

VKV

✂ cut on all dashed lines

▱ fold on all solid lines

íproco

conmutativa

Circle the operations that are commutative. (Encierra en un círculo las operaciones conmutativas.)

addition   subtraction

division   multiplication

propiedad

Find the reciprocal of each number. (Halla el recíproco de los siguientes números.)

$\dfrac{7}{12} =$ _____ $9 =$ _____

$1\dfrac{5}{8} =$ _____ $\dfrac{1}{6} =$ _____

Dinah Zike's
**Visual
Kinesthetic
Vocabulary**

cut on all dashed lines

fold on all solid lines

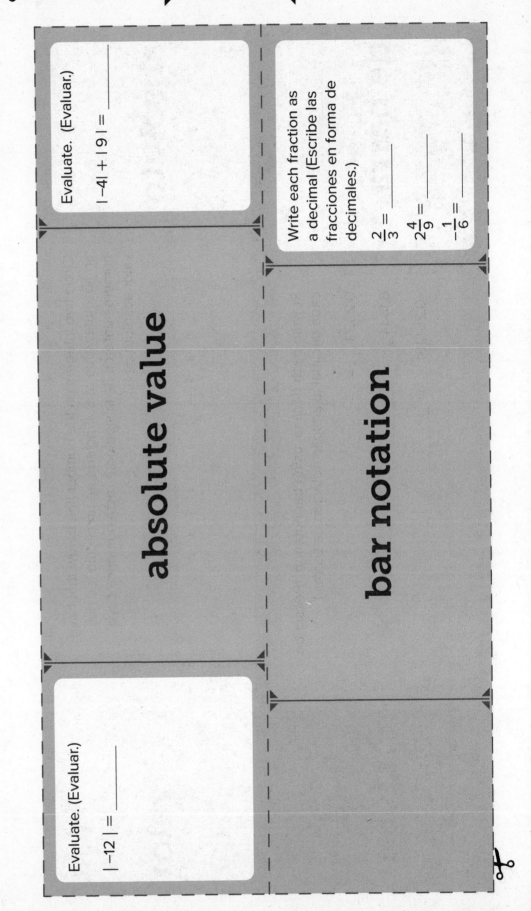

Evaluate. (Evaluar.)

$|-4| + |9| =$ _____

Write each fraction as a decimal (Escribe las fracciones en forma de decimales.)

$\frac{2}{3} =$ _____

$2\frac{4}{9} =$ _____

$-\frac{1}{6} =$ _____

absolute value

bar notation

Evaluate. (Evaluar.)

$|-12| =$ _____

cut on all dashed lines

fold on all solid lines

absoluto

Circle two integers on the number line below that have an absolute value of 8. (Encierra en un círculo los dos números enteros de la siguiente recta numérica cuyo valor absoluto es 8.)

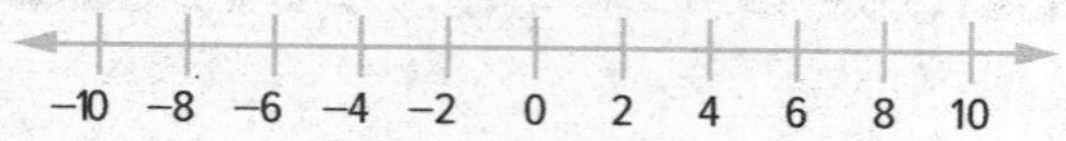

–10 –8 –6 –4 –2 0 2 4 6 8 10

valor

de barra

Rewrite each decimal using bar notation. (Reescribe cada decimal usando la notación de barras.)

0.2323 . . . = ________

6.1444 . . . = ________

–0.251251 . . . = ________

notación

Find the opposite of each integer. (Encuentra el opuesto de los siguientes enteros.)

12 _____ −5 _____ 23 _____

In what two quadrants are the signs of the coordinates the same? (¿En cuáles dos cuadrantes los signos de las coordenadas son iguales?) _____

opposites

quadrants

Dinah Zike's
VKV
Visual
Kinesthetic
Vocabulary

✂ cut on all dashed lines

▭ fold on all solid lines

es

uestos

Label Quadrants I, II, III, and IV.
(Rotula los cuadrantes I, II, III y IV.)

Why is the opposite of zero equal to zero? (¿Por qué el opuesto de cero
es cero?)

C

Define properties. (Define propiedades.)

Evaluate 12*m* if *m* = 3. (Evalúa 12*m* si *m* = 3.)

Define coefficient. (Define coeficiente.)

properties

evaluate

coefficient

iciente

r

iedades

Name the property that is shown in each example. (Nombra la propiedad que se muestra en los siguientes ejemplos.)

$56 + 0 = 56$

_____

$12 \cdot 5 = 5 \cdot 12$

_____

$3 + (6 + 4) = (3 + 6) + 4$

_____

What information do you need to be able to evaluate $6x + 3$? (¿Qué información necesitas para evaluar la ecuación $6x + 3$?)

Circle the coefficients in the expressions below. (Encierra en un círculo los coeficientes de las siguientes expresiones.)

$6x + 3 = 21$ $m - 3y$

$15 - 2p$ $24 + 3a = 9$

Dinah Zike's
Visual
Kinesthetic
Vocabulary

✂ cut on all dashed lines

▭ fold on all solid lines

Rewrite the expression 3x + x + x so that it has only one term. (Reescribe la expresión 3x + x + x de manera que tenga un único término.)

_____

expression

term

numérica

Simplify each numerical expression. (Simplifica las siguientes expresiones numéricas.)

$3 + 12 - (2 \times 3) =$ _____

$15 \div 3 + 20 - 8 =$ _____

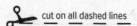
érmino

expresión

numerical

How many terms are in each expression? (¿Cuántos términos tienen las siguientes expresiones?)

x + 4 – 3y _____

9r + 4s – t _____

12 – 5a _____

m + m + m + m _____

Define numerical expression. (Define expresión numérica.)

Dinah Zike's
Visual Kinesthetic Vocabulary

 cut on all dashed lines

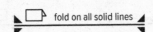 fold on all solid lines

Define equation. (Define ecuación.)

Circle the solution to each equation. (Encierra en un círculo la solución de las siguientes ecuaciones.)

$27 - y = 9$	14	16	18
$x + 52 = 100$	47	48	49
$36 \div m = 12$	2	3	4

What is the inverse operation of division? (¿Cuál es la operación inversa de la división?)

equation

solution

inverse operations

What is the inverse operation of addition? (¿Cuál es la operación inversa de la adición?)

Copyright © McGraw-Hill Education.

Visual Kinesthetic Learning   VKV21

Dinah Zike's
Visual
Kinesthetic
Vocabulary

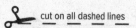

✂ cut on all dashed lines

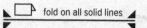

🔲 fold on all solid lines

inversas

ción

cuación

Solve each equation using inverse operations. (Utiliza las operaciones inversas para resolver las siguientes ecuaciones.)

$$x + 12 = 25$$

$$x = \underline{\hspace{2cm}}$$

$$16 = y - 3$$

$$\underline{\hspace{2cm}} = y$$

Define solution. (Define solución.)

Aiden bought 24 marbles for $6. Write and solve an equation to show how much each marble cost. (Andrés compró 24 canicas en $6. Escribe y resuelve una ecuación que muestre cuánto costó cada una.)

operaciones

Copyright © McGraw-Hill Education.

VKV22   **Visual Kinesthetic Learning**

✂ cut on all dashed lines

▭ fold on all solid lines

Define congruent. (Define congruente.)

List three polygons. Draw one example.
(Enumera tres polígonos. Dibuja un ejemplo.)

congruent

polygon

Dinah Zike's
Visual
Kinesthetic
Vocabulary

✂ cut on all dashed lines

▢ fold on all solid lines

ígono

e

Circle the two congruent figures. (Encierra en un círculo las dos figuras congruentes.)

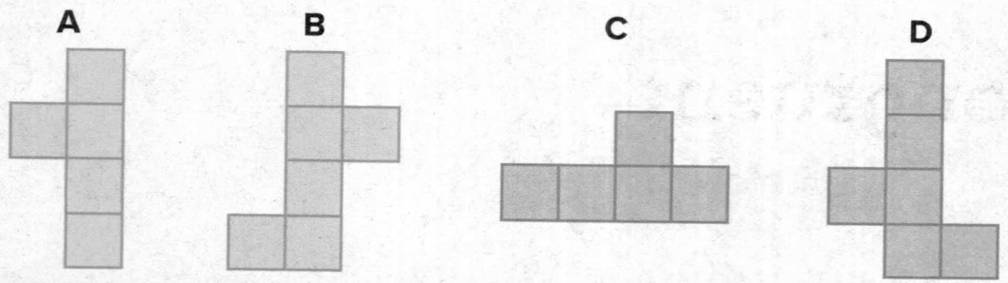

A   B   C   D

Explain why a circle is NOT a polygon. (Explica por qué un círculo NO es un polígono.)

✂ cut on all dashed lines   ⬒ fold on all solid lines

Define rhombus. (Define rombo.)

Circle the formula that represents the area of a parallelogram. (Encierra en un círculo la fórmula que representa el área de un paralelogramo)

$A = b^2 + h^2$ $A = 2(b + h)$ $A = bh$

rhombus

parallelogram

paralelogramo

Draw a pair of parallel lines. (Dibuja un par de rectas paralelas.)

ombo

Explain why a square is a rhombus. (Explica por qué un cuadrado es un rombo.)

Write about a time when you might need to know the surface area of an object. (Escribe sobre una situación en la cual podrías necesitar la superficie de un objeto.)

surface area

three-dimensional

Define surface area. (Define área de superficie.)

Draw a three-dimensional object. (Dibuja un objeto tridimensional.)

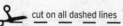

superficie

Find the surface area. (Calcula la superficie.)

$S.A. = 2\ell h + 2\ell w + 2hw$

15 cm

7 cm

2 cm

$S.A = $ _____

List the three dimensions. (Enumera las tres dimensiones.)

_____

_____

_____

_____ is the amount of space inside a three-dimensional figure, and it is measured in _____. (_____ es el espacio que se halla dentro de una figura tridimensional. Se mide en _____.)

área de

tri

✂ cut on all dashed lines

▭ fold on all solid lines

Define *vertex*. (Define *vértice*.)

Draw a triangular prism. (Dibuja un prisma triangular.)

vertex

rectangular

triangular prism

 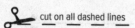
Draw a rectangular prism. (Dibuja un prisma rectangular.)

prisma triangular

rectangular

értice

The plural of vertex is vertices. How many vertices does the figure have? (¿Cuántos vértices tiene la figura?)

✂ cut on all dashed lines   ▢ fold on all solid lines

How is the median of a data set different from the mean? (¿Cuál es la diferencia entre la mediana y la media de un conjunto de datos?)

Define range. (Define rango.)

median

range

Dinah Zike's
Visual
Kinesthetic
Vocabulary

cut on all dashed lines

fold on all solid lines

O

a

Find the median of the data set below. (Halla la mediana del siguiente conjunto de datos.)

12 15 10 18 12 14 13 17 18

_____

Create a data set that has 6 numbers and a range of 12. (Crea una tabla de datos que tenga 6 números y un rango de 12.)

_____

_____

Dinah Zike's
Visual
Kinesthetic
Vocabulary

VKV

cut on all dashed lines

fold on all solid lines

interquartile

What is the interquartile range of the data set below?
(¿Cuál es el rango intercuartil del siguiente conjunto de datos?)

4   4   5   6   6   6   7   8   8   8

Dinah Zike's
Visual
Kinesthetic
Vocabulary

✁ cut on all dashed lines

⬚ fold on all solid lines

intercuartile

Circle the first and third quartiles in the data set below.
(Encierra en un círculo el primer y el tercer cuartiles en
el siguiente conjunto de datos.)

4   4   5   6   6   6   7   8   8   8

Dinah Zike's
Visual
Kinesthetic
Vocabulary

✂ ---- cut on all dashed lines

⬒ fold on all solid lines

If a data set has symmetric distribution, do you describe the center using the mean or median? Explain.(Si la distribución de un conjunto de datos es simétrica, ¿el centro se describe con la media o con la mediana? Explique.)

Define histogram. (Define histograma.)

symmetric

histogram

a

imétrico

In the space at right, draw an example of a histogram. (En el espacio de la derecha dibuja un ejemplo de histograma.)

Which line plot shows symmetric distribution? (¿Cuál gráfica de puntos presenta una distribución simétrica?)

A

Number of States Visited

```
    XXX
10
11  XXXXX
12  XXXXXX
13  XXX
14
15  X
16
17
18
19  X
20
```

B

Ages of Tennis Players (yr)

```
24
25  X
26  XXX
27  XXX
28  XXXX
29  XXXX
30  XXXX
31  XXX
32  XX
33  X
34
```

VKV Answer Appendix

VKV3

coordinate plane: See students' work for drawing. *graph*: See students' work.

VKV4

gráfica: See students' work.

VKV5

origin: See students' work.
ordered pair: 14; 3

VKV6

origen: the *x*- and *y*-axes intersect
par ordenado: (7, 11)

VKV7

y-coordinate: 18; 12; 65; 12.1
unit price: 5 tickets for $75

VKV8

coordinada-y: 4; 23; 5.9; 0.9
precio unitario: $22

VKV9

rational number: Sample answers: $\frac{12}{1}$; $\frac{35}{100}$; $3\frac{1}{10}$

VKV10

número racional: See students' work.

VKV11

Commutative Property: order
reciprocal: 8; $\frac{3}{4}$

VKV12

propiedad conmutativa: addition; multiplication
recíproco: $\frac{12}{7}$; $\frac{1}{9}$; $\frac{8}{13}$; $\frac{6}{1}$

VKV13

absolute value: 12; 13
bar notation: $0.\overline{6}$; $2.\overline{4}$; $-0.1\overline{6}$

VKV14

valor absoluto: See students' work.
notación de barra: $0.\overline{23}$; $6.1\overline{4}$; $-0.\overline{251}$

VKV15

opposites: −12; 5; −23
quadrants: I and III

VKV16

opuestos: Sample answer: 0 is neither negative nor positive.
cuadrantes: See students' work for labels.

VKV17

coefficient: See students' work.
evaluate: 36
properties: See students' work.

VKV18

coeficiente: 6; 1 and −3; −2; 3
evaluar: Sample answer: the value of *x*
propiedades: Additive Identity; Commutative; Associative

VKV19

expression: 9; 17
term: 5*x*

VKV20

expresión: See students' work.
término: 3; 2; 3; 4

VKV21

equation: See students' work.
inverse operations: subtraction; multiplication
solution: 18; 48; 3

VKV22

ecuación: 24*x* = $6; $0.25 per marble
operaciones inversas: 13; 19
solución: See students' work.

VKV23

congruent: See students' work.

polygon: Sample answer: triangle, square, rectangle; See students' work.

VKV24

congruente: A and C

polígono: Sample answer: a circle does not have any straight line segments.

VKV25

parallelogram: $A = bh$

rhombus: See students' work.

VKV26

paralelogramo: See students' work for drawing.

rombo: Sample answer: a rhombus is defined as a parallelogram with four congruent sides, which a square has, therefore a square is a kind of rhombus.

VKV27

three-dimensional: See students' work for drawing.

surface area: See students' work for both exercises.

VKV28

tridimensional: length, width, height, volume, cubic units

área de superficie: 298cm^2

VKV29

triangular prism: See students' work for drawing.

vertex: See students' work.

VKV30

prisma triangular: See students' work for drawing.

vértices: 5

VKV31

median: Sample answer: the median is the number that falls in the middle of an ordered list of numbers, the mean requires adding up all numbers and dividing by the number of data.

mode: See students' work.

range: See students' work.

VKV32

mediana: 14

moda: 2

rango: Sample answer: 3, 3, 6, 7, 10, 15

VKV33

interquartile: 3

VKV34

intercuartile: 5; 8

VKV35

histogram: See students' work.

symmetric: mean; See students' work

VKV36

histograma: See students' work for drawing.

simétrico: B